# The Power to Change

**Creating the Life You Want Through Healthy Choices**

# The Power to Change

**Creating the Life You Want Through Healthy Choices**

**By Eric Gillman**

"This is the book to overcome inertia in your life and build momentum to achieving your goals and realizing your dreams. In life, stories of overcoming long odds to survive or thrive are impressive, but perhaps more impressive is a story of overcoming average, overcoming satisfied, or overcoming good enough. Eric's book, *The Power to Change,* encourages those who are wondering why they are just getting by and inspires them to achieve monumental success, make an enormous difference, and win the game of life. Powerful lesson taught with simple strategies and heartwarming stories. This book – and the author – are winners."

~ Michael J. Maher, two-time #1 Bestselling Author, North America's Most Referred Real Estate Professional, and founder of The Generosity Generation.

Dedicated to my loving mom. Thank you for always being there for me, and supporting me, even when it seemed like you were not. You never stopped caring and it has made me into the person I am today.

# Table of Contents

# Foreword
### by Barry Gillman (aka Eric's Dad)

I've observed personalities don't change very much as the child grows into the adult. What you see in kindergarten is usually pretty much what you get as an adult.

At 6, Eric was funny, social, good-looking, and athletic. A friend of ours described him as "a big grin surrounded by a small boy". At 10, he was always the class clown: so funny and photogenic that he was featured in a Rosie O'Donnell national TV special "Kids are Punny".

But faced with a problem, he'd always take the easy way out. He morphed into a sullen teenager (yes I know, they all do that), but obese, lazy, and getting into all kinds of trouble both in school and outside.

Somewhere in that distressed and distressing teenager, there was a spark of determination and motivation that burned, slowly at first, and with some flickering, but it never went out.

There's an old joke: how many psychologists does it take to change a lightbulb? Only one, but first the lightbulb has to want to change. Well, Eric wanted to change. We didn't believe it at first. That this overweight, argumentative teen would become a triathlon athlete and a motivational speaker...you had to be kidding.

The message I'd share with readers of this book is that if you want it badly enough, you can do it. The determination to change can be kindled quickly, but the process of change may take many years. We watched for a decade while Eric battled his own bad habits and built a successful and healthy life. We offered plenty of advice and admonitions, but in the end, that determination and motivation could only come from within him.

I recall planning to watch 15-year-old Eric's high school football practice. I asked him "There are 50 kids all in identical uniforms, how will I know which is you?" "I'll be the fat one trailing 50 yards behind the rest", said Eric, "but I'll still be running". And he still is.

# Prelude

Do you feel like you could be achieving more out of life, but don't know how?

Sometimes we find ourselves in a place where it's difficult to look at the person in the mirror and feel great about who is looking back at you. You may look at yourself and wonder: "How did I get this way?" or even "How did I let it get this bad?" There is no greater disappointment than being disappointed in yourself, and in letting other people down. I have seen that face in the mirror far too many times in my life, and maybe you have as well.

We live in a world of excess and countless personal choices, and with so many of these options in life it is often hard to make the right ones.

Thank you for choosing to open this book and start reading. This choice might be the first on a path towards your own further greatness. We all are capable of achieving remarkable things in our lives, but we might not even realize it. Whether or not you know it, you are just as worthy, capable and deserving of achieving anything you want as anyone else in this world. This book will provide you with the simple tools to unlock your true potential and enact positive and long-lasting change in any area of your life.

In this book you will discover:

- Where you are in life is because of the choices you have made in the past, but where you are going depends completely on the choice you make today.

- The ability to realize, visualize and unlock your true potential.

- The simple and easy to apply concepts that you can use immediately to enact long-lasting change within any area of your life.

Every day we are bombarded with choices of how to live our lives. We choose what to wear, what to eat, and with whom and where we do so. Almost every moment in our lives brings some type of choice. Red shirt or blue shirt, oatmeal or hash browns, to go to school or not go to school.

We have all made some great choices in our lives and we can all look back on those moments and be proud of them. At the same time, we have all made decisions in the past that either we regretted, or had a negative effect on the lives we are living.

**The main message you will find in this book is: where we are right now in life is because of the choices we made in the past, but where we are going depends entirely on who we choose to be now and in the future.**

Do you ever feel like you could be achieving more out of life, but don't know exactly how? We have an innate urge to be great. There is a voice within all of us that cries out to do or be something bigger. Maybe that voice is very loud, or maybe it has been silenced by fear. Either way, it is there. It is your unlimited potential, and far too often we ignore our potentials and go through life living lives of quiet desperation.

Have you made it to a point in your life where you are ready for some change in any or all significant areas of your life? Have you gotten sick and tired of looking at the person in the mirror, and knowing that there is something greater there? Do you know what absolutely incredible things you are capable of in this life?

Many years before this book was written I was a person who was tired of looking at that sad face of disappointment. I was ready for some change and I didn't even know it. You might be ready for some change as well, whether or not you know it.

Thank you for taking a moment to pick up this book and read the first couple of pages. I hope that through this experience I can share with you the tools to create the life of your dreams through making healthy choices.

# Introduction

On 6/6/06 I was expelled from school, on the last day of my junior year in high school.

It ended up being one of the best things that ever happened to me.

I'll come right out and say it: I am a record breaker. I hold some records I want to share with you that might give you a bit of insight into the person I am. My records aren't conventional, and I would bet most people would be hard-pressed to attempt them. I am not necessarily proud of all of them, but they have defined the person I am, and brought me to be the person to write this book.

In my high school I set the record for the slowest "40 time." For those of you who don't know, that is a 40-meter dash run by football players. I also held the record of my middle-school class for most school suspensions. I even had the record for most penalties and longest suspension on my ice hockey team.

All of these problems stemmed from my own insecurities. Looking at me now you would never know, but going into high school I was 5'7" and weighed just under 250 lbs. Check out the page in the back of the book! ☺

I was a big boy and I liked to party, and by party I mean sit home every weekend watching movies and eating pizza alone. I spent the majority of my young life making unhealthy choices.

Choices like getting bacon on my bagel with cream cheese every morning, or eating three full cups of whipped cream to win a 25-cent bet.

Sometimes I made a healthy choice, like drinking a Slim Fast shake, but unfortunately I would be drinking it as a milkshake with my lunch, which made it not so healthy. I would sometimes make the healthy choice to go to the gym, and then follow it with the unhealthy choice of going to 7-11 and getting a large Slurpee.

When I say the term "healthy choices," your first thought is probably about what you eat, and that concern is significant, but healthy choices go much further than that.

Choices are something we all face every day. As I suggested above, whether you realize it or not, you make thousands of choices every single day, both consciously and unconsciously.

From the moment you open your eyes in the morning, you make the decision whether or not to get out of bed, or stay in and snooze for a few more minutes.

From that moment on, it is a nonstop barrage of choices to be made throughout the day. Some of them are so minor you don't even notice, like the choice to walk a certain way, or the choice of when to inhale and exhale.

However, it is the bigger choices we make that can have a lifetime impact on the person we become. If you look at a person, they are simply the summation of all the different life choices they have made thus far.

What choices have you made in the past that made you into the person you are today? Are they things you are proud of, or things whose effects you want to change in your life? Often, we get caught up in a world of unhealthy choices, and we follow the path that is the easiest and simplest. Commonly, most people don't realize that one decision, which might seem minor at the time, can have a profound effect on the trajectory of their entire life.

I made a lot of unhealthy choices in my life, and it didn't stop with just food. A great mentor of mine once taught me: "How you do something is how you do everything."

For me this was clearly true. The unhealthy choices I made for my health spilled over to unhealthy choices in other parts of my life.

I might hold the record for the slowest 40 time, but I also held the record for most school suspensions in my whole 8$^{th}$-grade class. In 8th grade I once was suspended for putting laxative in someone's drink as a practical joke.

At the time I thought it was funny, and honestly never thought much of it. I know it might even sound funny to a few of you, and for those few—just don't.

Making unhealthy choices led me to smoke my first cigarette in 7th grade and buy my first dime bag in 8th. The ironic thing about that was that when we went to smoke the first cigarette in the park after school, we already had the cigarettes—but no one would sell a bunch of 13-year old kids a lighter.

Making unhealthy choices led me to being detained by the police when I was 14, and then those same types of choices led me to know what handcuffs felt like at the age of 16. Drinking, drugs, trespassing and vandalism were all familiar to me in my formative years. By the time I was 18 my mom was in tears when she told me that it killed her knowing her youngest son was going to die or go to prison before he even got the chance to go to college.

This trend didn't stop—all throughout high school I was always the troublemaker. Always seemed to be at the front of the line when it came to doing something stupid.

Now I wasn't some bona fide badass or anything; more like a class clown who knew how to influence people—a teacher's worst nightmare.

All of these shenanigans led to me getting expelled my last day of my junior year, 6/6/06—it was an evil day. However, in hindsight it ended up being one of the better things to happen to me.

Though there was a specific event that led to my being expelled, which I'll tell you about later, I wasn't really expelled for that one thing. I got in trouble for almost everything and it was just the last straw. Drinking at dances, cheating, lying to teachers, selling drugs on campus, skipping school, you name it—I was always down for trouble, and usually leading the way.

I was asked to leave the school because of the person I was and the choices I was making. You would think that would be enough for me to change. Nope.

I kept on the path of self-destruction throughout my whole senior year at a new high school. I kept selling drugs, kept going to Tijuana on the weekends and telling my parents I was going to a friend's house or out to a party.

So now you're probably wondering—what the hell should I be listening to this guy for? He sounds like he was nothing but a fat, cheating, washed-up drug dealer loser.

I always wanted big things in life. There was a voice in my head that told me that I was destined for big things in this world—but I didn't know what they were, or how to achieve them. I lacked purpose and direction. So I just did what felt good and right at the time. I had a bad circle of influence and enough drive—in the wrong direction—to sink the Titanic.

Have you ever felt this way before? Like you know that you are capable of achieving great things, or at least better things than those happening right now, but for whatever reason it seems you can't make them happen?

I would like to share with you today what caused my life to change, and then give you the tools that I used, so you can instigate change in your own life as well. It's my belief that if you pave a rocky road in your own life, then it's your responsibility to turn back and help others smooth their own rocky paths.

So when did it change for me? When did I wake up? I will tell you that it wasn't easy, and it was not overnight. I would love to say that one day I just woke up and my life 180ed, and I became this new perfect version of myself. This is not the truth for me, and for almost anyone you talk to who has gone through some type of life transformation, not the reality for him or her either.

Some people believe that sudden and drastic change is completely necessary for a change of course in their lives. That might be true for some people, but for most people who want lasting and permanent change, they must make small changes every day and stick to them. Small, constant corrections on your course will eventually get you to your destination, on target.

When a plane takes off from one place to go to another it has a flight plan. But the majority of what the pilot does is make minor course corrections as the plane travels along its journey. Even the smallest deviation from the flight plan, gone uncorrected by the pilot, could lead the plane to a completely different destination. Similarly in life, one seemingly minor decision made today that goes uncorrected can send your life path down an entirely different trajectory.

We live in a society where everything comes so instantly. High-speed Internet, "FastPass," quickie marts and instant coffee have our minds convinced that success and gratification can come instantly. This is not true when it comes to change in your life.

The process for lasting change in your life is always slow and gradual, not drastic. A little bit of progress, through making healthy choices every day, is what will allow you to create the life of your dreams.

If you want lasting change in your life, you must start by making small choices in the right direction EVERY DAY. Constantly move yourself closer to the life you desire by making these small strides EVERY DAY. Small changes made constantly EVERY DAY will eventually become the massive change that you desire out of your life.

**First we must accept the fact that where we are right now in life is a result of the person we were and the choices we made in the past, but where we are going depends entirely on who we CHOOSE to be from now on.** Up to this point, you are currently the sum of the choices you have made in life. If you want to change the person you see in the mirror, ask yourself; "What changes am I willing to make TODAY to change the rest of my life?"

# CHAPTER 1
# Harnessing the Power of a Decision

"There's no reason to have a plan B because it distracts from plan A."

**Will Smith, two-time Academy Award winning actor**

"To make a decision means to cut off the other option. Once you have truly harnessed the power of a decision, the other option no longer exists."

**– Eric Gillman**

We have complete control over almost every aspect of our lives, as soon as we harness the power of truly making a decision.

When you make a decision to do something you must cut off the other option. The word *decision* comes from the Latin root word *decidere,* which means to cut off, to sever. When you truly DECIDE to do something you are effectively saying, "There is no other alternative to do what I have decided to do."

"It is in your moments of decision that your destiny is shaped."

**– Tony Robbins, World famous motivational speaker**

1

Imagine you are walking down a road and suddenly you come to a fork. You have to choose to bear right or bear left, and that will determine the place that you end up. When you decide which road to travel, the other road is blocked off completely and no longer exists as an option. For example, if you choose to work out every day of the year, then the option of not doing so is no longer there. If you decide to make a mark in a certain class, the option to fail no longer exists, and you should act as if that's the only possible course.

When I was 16 years old I made the decision to be a healthier person—my life makes clear that you have that same ability to change anything in your life, starting right now!

People often ask me, "Eric, what made your life change?" The truth is, it was the day I chose to be different, the day I chose to declare: this was not going to be the life for me. I was sick and tired of looking in the mirror and being disgusted with the person looking back at me. I made a few very important decisions in my life that shaped me to become the person I am today; those decisions did not all come at once. Initially I decided to get my body healthy, but it wasn't until years later I made other difficult decisions to get my mind to follow. I can't emphasize enough: small choices every day have a huge effect on the direction of your life. One small choice today—and moving from there—could mean something potentially huge down the road.

By the age of 16 I was obese, unhealthy, and had formed a destructive lifestyle for myself, and for anyone around me. I decided not to be that person anymore.

What decisions are you ready to make in your life that will define the person you will become tomorrow? Have you ever felt stuck in your circumstances? I used to think that being big was my destiny. When I was younger I accepted that I was going to be overweight for the rest of my life. Have you ever felt that your circumstances limited outweigh your options? The truth of the matter is: YOU are in complete control of your life. But in order to take the wheel of your own destiny you MUST accept that you have the power to choose what you focus on. Acknowledge that you have the power to influence your circumstances.

The change from that point on can be drastic or it can be gradual. The point is, the choice has been made, and by you. There were many, many choices I had to make that led me here today and two in particular I would like to share with you. My hope is that by sharing my story with you, you might draw some similarities in your life, and you can open your eyes to see that where you are in life right now is only temporary. You can change the direction of your life—today—by the choices you decide to make.

My first choice was to get healthy, and the second was the choice to take control of the rest of my life. They came years apart, but both during high school and both equally important.

The interesting thing about the changes in my life is that it wasn't my successes that made me successful in life, but my failures that led me there. We must first learn to fail forward towards our goals. Fail your way forward to the person you want to become.

# CHAPTER 2
# Fail Your Way to Success

**"You miss 100% of the shots you don't take."**

**– Wayne Gretzky, Ice Hockey legend and MVP**

**Have you ever felt like you can achieve more out of life—but don't know how?**

Let's face it, you probably won't achieve every single goal you set out to accomplish. This is OK. In fact, it is great. If we lived in a world where everything was easy to achieve, then no one would push themselves or others to become better people.

In order to be successful in anything, you must learn to let go of your fear of failure, and instead embrace it as part of the process. Achieving goals in any aspect of your life is a *process,* not an event.

So often we see success as an event in someone's life, but we rarely ever catch a glimpse of what got him or her there. We see the championship team take the trophy, or the student graduate at the top of their class, and for so many of us we think that it is just something that happened to that person because of who they were, or how lucky they are.

What we so often do *not* see is the championship team in training every day, working hard, getting hurt, and losing important games. We see a championship team and believe they are lucky to be there. We do not see the student reading at all hours of the day, working while going to school, failing to finish key assignments and sleeping in the library. We see the top graduate and think that it was simply because that's "just who they are." It's this type of thinking that allows us to believe we are stuck in our own circumstances (and that keeps us there), and that certain people are destined to be more successful.

I'll say it again, because it's that important: Success is a process, not an event, and in order to be successful we must learn to embrace this process. The key part of this process is the failures you will experience along the way.

**"Let me tell you something you already know. The world ain't all sunshine and rainbows. It's a very mean and nasty place, and I don't care how tough you are, it will beat you to your knees and keep you there permanently if you let it. You, me or nobody is gonna hit as hard as life. But it ain't about how hard you hit, it's about how hard you can get hit and keep moving forward, how much you can take and keep moving forward. That's how winning is done! Now if you know what you're worth, then go out and get what you're worth, but you gotta be willing to take the hits, and not pointing fingers saying you ain't where you wanna be because of him or her or anybody. Cowards do that, and that ain't you! You're better than that."**

**– Rocky Balboa**

**"People are rewarded in public for what they practice for years in private."**

**– Tony Robbins**

# CHAPTER 3
# THINK BIG and Don't be Afraid to Miss

**"You must do the thing you think you cannot do"**
        **- Eleanor Roosevelt, Former first lady of the United States**

**"Success is not final, failure is not fatal: it is the courage to continue that counts."**
**– Winston Churchill, Former Prime Minister of the United Kingdom**

A goal should be something realistic and obtainable, and it should be something that is going to push you to grow as a person. It should be something that causes you to **step out of your comfort zone** and give yourself the chance to fail and try again—but not give up on what you truly want, even before you have tried.

Most people walk around with an immense amount of fear of failing on a goal that they want to achieve. This fear can be crippling for them and can even stop them from trying to attempt the goal in the first place. Fear causes people to make excuses for what they truly want in life.

You must learn to accept failure as part of life and learning. No one was ever great the first time they ever tried anything. The people who became the greatest were also the ones who failed the most and kept trying the most.

When Michael Jordan was 14 years old he was cut from his middle-school basketball team. He went home that night, locked himself in his room and cried. He had the opportunity to give up right there and never play basketball again. But as we all know he did quite the opposite. Michael Jordan had a goal, with urgency. He never did give up, but instead went on to be one of the greatest basketball players ever. Imagine if he only tried one time in middle school and then gave up?

Walt Disney, Oprah, and Thomas Edison all were people who failed many times in their lives, on their way to greatness. What makes them remarkable people is not only what they accomplished in life, but that they did not give up on what they wanted and were not afraid to fail.

Have you ever told yourself you can't do something before you even tried? Have you ever labeled yourself not able to do something before you even started? Now is the time to change that. RIGHT NOW! **Do not ever let fear of failure rob you of the divine satisfaction it is to achieve something great.**

In order to be successful in any area of your life you must accept this truth: **In order to have success in the future, you must be willing to fail forward toward it today.** What that means is that your path to success will not be easy. Remember, nothing worth having is easy to get.

As I outlined above, you can look at a successful person in any walk of life and claim that they "have it easy," or "they are just born to have that, or to be that way." While this is an easy assumption to make, it could not be further from the truth.

When you see someone who has been successful, you are seeing the culmination of years of hard work, dedication and past failures. **Every moment of success is built upon a mountainous foundation of failure before it.** People who have achieved great things in life are not necessarily better people than anyone else, but they have proven they can endure, over more time than anyone else. They are the ones who take failure as a *suggestion,* not an answer. **On the road to success, people who succeed see failures as a pit stop on the journey, not the end destination.**

So many people want more out of their lives, and maybe they make strides to get there, but so many people hit the first wall of failure and let it stop them dead. In order to be successful you must bust through that wall and keep moving forward.

What things in your life have you attempted and failed, and let failure be the answer? What are you missing out on by letting fear of failure stop you from even trying?

We are all capable of doing great things, but sadly, most of us never do. Even sadder than that is the reason why we never do—because we convince ourselves we are not able to do it. We are all capable of achieving anything that we put our minds to, but so many times we convince ourselves we can't do something before we even try.

# CHAPTER 4
# The Marathoner Who Couldn't Run a Mile...

**"There is no such thing as failure. There are only results."**
**– Tony Robbins, World famous motivational speaker**

I would like to share a story with you about a personal experience of mine where I learned this lesson all too well.

As you heard earlier, I wasn't exactly born an "athlete," or for that matter anything close to it. I had to work hard just to become average. When you start from rock bottom, the only place to go from there is up. That's where I wanted to move, but like so many people I didn't know how.

Has anyone had to run a mile for gym class before? When I was in 6th grade that dreaded day came and I was disqualified. Let me share with you a quick story of what is possible when you put your mind to something.

When I was 12 years old—and weighed over 210 pounds—I would have told you that it was impossible for me to run more than a mile.

We have all been there before, the day in gym class where we are required to run a mile. This is a simple task that most kids shouldn't have too much trouble with. When I was growing up, it was a pretty standard test for most kids.

When I was in the 6th grade, this dismal day fell upon me. I was so out of shape that I had been dreading this day the entire semester. I might have even tried to make up some lame excuse for not running it, but the coaches were not accepting any of that. I knew that it was time to face the music and there was no excuse that was going to get me out of this required event.

We lined up for the first of twelve laps around the gym track to complete the full mile. The teacher told us the average expected time was about 10 minutes, but we should just try our best. So the whistle blew and we took off like a bullet out of a gun, or for me, more like a bowling ball through molasses.

I was never any speed demon, but this day was particularly embarrassing. It only took three laps before I started to get lapped by the faster kids in the class.

One by one the other kids were finishing the mile—8 minutes, 9 minutes, 10 minutes. I kept trucking along, but after seven laps I found it hard to even keep running at all. I slowed to a walk, a solid full lap behind the next person. I knew I wasn't doing great, but that became sharply clear to me when I heard the shrill whistle blow and the coach yell, "bring it in." Part of me was relieved, but also distressed over why I wasn't allowed to walk through the finish.

After the class ended I went to the coach and asked if I had a recorded time, to which she responded that I was disqualified and deemed "NA," which stood for "Not Able." At the age of 12, I had been labeled as unable to complete a physical task that every single person in my class was able to do. Before, I had been picked last to be on a team, but this was like being the last pick and both captains passing over you anyways.

This event killed my self-esteem. I now thought it was impossible to run, let alone a whole mile. This thought became my reality, and I basically gave up on running, and most physical activity. I remember thinking to myself, "It's impossible for me to run a mile, so why even try?"

Reinforcing what I said before, have you ever talked yourself out of doing something, simply because you thought you might not be good at it? Maybe it was a sport, or a class, or talking to that girl or guy you liked. Everyone has done it at some point. It's all right, because that's how our mind protects us from getting hurt, physically or emotionally. However, it is this same defense mechanism that holds us back from growing to become a better person. We are all capable of achieving greatness in any desired area, but it is this innate, fear-based reaction that shields us from becoming the person we truly desire to be.

For me, this went on for years. Thinking I was incapable of running and always shrugging it off as "not my thing." I would hear stories of people doing 10Ks and marathons, but I told myself that it simply wasn't something I was going to accomplish—until one day I had a chat with a friend who changed everything for me. I'll tell you more about that later. For now, I'll tell you that I chose to embrace failure as part of the process, to fail forward toward my goal.

Don't let the fear of failure paralyze you from pursuing something you are passionate about. You are capable of amazing things, but might not know how yet. That is what I hope to share with you in this book.

**TRUTH: "You are just as worthy, deserving, and capable of achieving everything you want as any other person on earth."**

**– Hal Elrod, International keynote speaker**
**and NY Times best-selling author**

# CHAPTER 5
# What Do You Want?

**"Change your thoughts and you change your world"**
**–Norman Vincent Peale, Author "Positive Thinking"**

Think of one thing you **truly** want to achieve. Some goal, some vision, something you want as a part of your life. What would it mean to you to get this thing? How would it make you feel? This could be an object, a place, or maybe just a general feeling of well-being. I want you to think about this right now, and write it down below. In an ideal world, what is something you want to achieve in your life? It can be big or small. Maybe it's not even an achievement, but just something you want to change in your life, but by doing so it will have a massive effect on your life and perhaps the lives of others.

SOMETHING I WANT TO ACHIEVE:

_____

Now ask yourself: what will it take to get this thing? What actions will I have to take to get it? What habits will I have to change or what habits must I begin to make this a part of my life? What will it mean to me to get it?

These are all important questions to ask yourself when considering a goal that you want to pursue. Knowing what you want and chasing after it is what life is truly all about. We are born to chase our dreams and make them a reality. Continue to consider all the things you must do to make this goal become a reality. What does it mean to you to achieve the goals that you want, and how would you feel if it happened?

Whatever actions you must take, think about each one of them. What specific actions need to take place in order to start moving towards that goal. Maybe there are a lot of things you need to do, maybe there are just one or two. For right now just think about the first action step you can take that you KNOW will make you move closer to the goal you wrote down above. Now ask yourself: if I try to do these things and I succeed, what will that look like? How great would it feel to pass that class, or drop that weight, or get that job, or make that team, or ask out that person in your class? Maybe your goal isn't even that big. Maybe you just want to stop being sick of looking at the person in the mirror. I know that was motivation for me.

Now consider this: if you take massive action towards your goals, and things don't pan out exactly how you want them, how will your life be affected?

**If you go for something big in your life and come up short, you will always be further ahead of where you would be if you never started at all.**

**Remember, it is all about the process. "Every day a little bit stronger, a little bit smarter; every day is the best day of my life."**

If you are constantly going for big things and failing, you are always moving closer to your goal. Anyone who has achieved something great in life will tell you that getting to that moment took countless failed attempts. Maybe they only got it perfect once or twice in their life, out of millions of attempts. People will be seen and remembered for their finished products. They are seen only at the top, but never on the journey. In order to do something great we must be ready to fail, fail, and fail some more.

**Fail your way to the top**: Consider Thomas A. Edison, one of the world's greatest inventors, responsible for the invention of the incandescent light bulb. Without this crowning achievement we could still be sitting in a candlelit world of darkness, but Edison changed that. While you might think that Edison invented the light bulb in his free time while inventing other things, you could not be more wrong.

Prior to the invention and patent of his light bulb, Edison had over 10,000 documented failed attempts at creating it. He tried, he failed, and he did it 9,999 more times. How many times have you ever tried to accomplish something difficult in your life? If you fail, maybe you try again, possibly one more time, but after that you give up. This is why, I am sorry to say this, no one will remember you for that attempt.

Edison, when asked about his numerous failures, had this to say; "I did not fail 10,000 times, I merely found 10,000 ways how to not make a light bulb."

What would the world be like today if everyone accepted failure as the end of the road? What would the world be like if Edison quit on his 7,000th attempt? What would basketball be like if Michael Jordan stayed locked up in his room crying and never took a jump shot again? The point is that they did not stop, and neither should you. You are just as worthy, capable and deserving of greatness as Thomas Edison and Michael Jordan. But first you must prove to the world that you **DO NOT LET FAILURE BE YOUR ANSWER, MERELY A SUGGESTION ON THE ROAD TO GREATNESS.**

What will the world of tomorrow be like if you let failure be the answer to your problems today? Let's not rob the rest of the world of the greatness that is born within each of us. We are all capable of achieving great things in our own lives. First you must accept this, and then move step by step towards that goal.

# CHAPTER 6
# One More Game for the Rest of Your Life:  Failing Forward to Greatness

"I've missed more than 9,000 shots in my career. I've lost almost 300 games. Twenty-six times, I've been trusted to take the game winning shot and missed. I've failed over and over and over again in my life. And that is why I succeed."

> – Michael Jordan, Six-time NBA champion
> and five-time NBA MVP

"There are no secrets to success. It is the result of preparation, hard work and learning from failure"

> – Colin Powell, Former Secretary General of the United States

"The difference between a successful person and others is not a lack of strength, not a lack of knowledge, but rather in a lack of will."

> – Vince Lombardi, Hall of fame NFL coaching legend

"You can achieve everything you want out of life, once you help enough people achieve what they want out of life."

> – Eric Gillman

You might be wondering how a kid who couldn't break six seconds on a forty-yard dash would then be selected to play among the county's very best athletes. In 2007 I had the privilege of playing in the San Diego County high school All Star game. I would love to tell you that I became some type of super athlete over my high school career, and they had no choice but to put me into the game, but that is not the way it happened. Here is the story of how, through helping others, and failing forward, I was able to play in the greatest game I ever participated in.

After three years of football at my high school I was able to work myself into a decent football player. I might not have been the best, but I was no longer the worst on the team. Every day after practice I would work just a little bit more, building my body and my mind. I would repeat these words to myself constantly:

"Every day a little bit faster, every day a little bit stronger ... every day."

I learned a life lesson early on in my football career that goes way beyond the football field: nothing in life worth having is easy to get. So I worked at it, bit by bit, every day. I changed my diet and lost weight. I changed my workouts and got stronger. All of this in an effort to live out a dream I had for three years, to be a starting player on my high school varsity team. It was a dream I wanted more than anything. Have you ever dreamed of something so much, and wanted it so badly that when you think about it you can feel it? It's that feeling that wakes you up early in the morning and keeps your mind racing late at night.

We all have things in our lives that we strive for, whether it's making a team, getting a date, passing a class, getting along with family, getting the new job, or even just surviving the day. For me it was starting on that field every Friday night.

So my junior year I put in the work all year, and felt I was ready to take on my senior year of school and football. You know how sometimes you feel like you have a complete handle on life, like everything is in control, and then suddenly, sometimes with no warning, your whole life changes and your foundation is rocked? Well on June 6th, 2006 my foundation rocked so much that everything that I built collapsed.

As I suggested early in the book, I was expelled from my high school on my very last day of my junior year. What did I get expelled for? I mindlessly used my calculator on two questions of the non-calculator section of my math final. When my teacher confronted me about it I made one of the biggest mistakes of my life: I lied about it, trying to pass it off. It all happened so quickly; I didn't know what I was thinking.

As I alluded, the truth of the matter was that this wasn't this sole reason I was asked to leave the school. It was simply the straw that broke the camel's back. In hindsight I can't blame them for their actions. It was my unhealthy choices that led me to that point, and on 6/6/06 it was time to pay the piper.

In a single day I felt like I had lost everything. I felt a deep sense of emptiness. I saw so many things in front of me disappear; my heart ached. Where would I go? Would I still get into college? What will my friends and family think of this?

So I was able to find another high school to take me in for my senior year, the San Diego Jewish Academy. Soon after being accepted into the school on a probationary status, I looked to see if I could still play football. The school I had moved to had a football program, but it was not nearly the caliber of my old school. The issue was not if I could physically play for them, but if I was eligible.

In San Diego County the CIF (California Interscholastic Federation) had a rule that when a student transferred schools, that student is ineligible to play any varsity sports he had played the year before. This was a rule put into place to stop big high schools from recruiting the best players to play at their schools. Since I had played football the year before, I was now ineligible to play for my new school.

The only practical way to get around this problem was by filing a hardship claim with the CIF. It helped that the one person on the faculty at my old school who had seen my positive attitude was the football coach, and the moment he got the news that I was being expelled he went right to work to file the hardship claim. This move had nothing to do with sports, so we figured that an exception would be made. The process would take 4–6 weeks, so I started practicing with my new team, hoping for a good result.

As a new addition, I wanted to earn the respect of the other players, so I went to almost every single summer workout. My new team was not very hard to impress. They were playing in the eight-man football league, and within that league ranked as #13 out of 13 teams. I love and respect everyone who played in that program, but the fact is, they weren't very good. Many factors played into this but mainly it was due to being a small school, with an undeveloped program for Jewish boys who were more focused on academics than athletics—great for future careers but not exactly a coach's recipe for a football championship. Regardless of the team's status, I was just happy I got a chance to put the pads on.

So after a long summer of hard workouts we got the news back from my hardship claim. It was denied. Again I felt knocked down, but not defeated. We still had one more chance. We could file an appeal, which we did.

At this point the pre-season games had started, so time was of the essence. I would practice with the team every day, but come game day, I was on the sidelines helping to keep the players in the game and motivated.

My appeal date was set 30 days out, so I missed our first four games of the official season. In October I attended the appeal hearing. With me came my father and both football coaches from each of the schools. We went into the meeting fully prepared to explain that my switching schools had absolutely nothing to do with football, and thus I should be eligible to play for the remainder of the season.

I went home that night feeling good about the meeting and thinking that there is no way they wouldn't understand it. I have to be able to play; I had been working towards this all of high school. Forty-eight hours later we got a phone call and my dad answered. He walked into my room and told me that my appeal had been denied. It felt like I got stabbed in the heart with an icicle.

The rug was swept out from under me again and I felt my first taste of rock bottom. I didn't know what to do.

The next day I went to school and saw my football coach. He greeted me and expressed his sympathy for my situation. None of us could really make much sense of it, but at that point it did not matter. The decision was final and there were no more moves to make. I would not be able to play football my senior year of high school.

For those of you reading this who have never touched a pigskin in your life, or played any sports for that matter, think of it like this: Is there something in your life you love? A skill or hobby you have been working on for years? Something that is not only what you do, but who you are? Sports, videogames, watching movies, going out with friends, writing, working with wood or working on cars. Imagine if tomorrow, with no warning, for no valid reason that makes sense to you, that thing was taken away from you, for the rest of your entire life. How would that make you feel?

I felt empty. I felt I had lost purpose. I sat in my room feeling like an empty shell of a bullet that had just been fired.

High school football is a unique sport for young people because unlike other sports such as soccer, basketball, volleyball or baseball, there are no young adult football leagues. Unless you go on to play college football, which was not in the cards for me, high school is the final stop in your career. That is part of what makes it so special for so many young men.

So I sat in my football coach's office in an eerie dead silence after we discussed the news. He then offered me two options. Since I was no longer eligible to play in any games, he suggested that there was no more reason for me to practice. He gave the option to hang up my pads for the season—effectively forever—or I could stay on and continue to practice with my teammates. I wasn't going to let failure be the end of my road, so I decided to keep playing.

Sometimes when life gives you lemons you have to make lemonade, and that's what I did. I did the only thing I could do at that point: keep moving forward. On your road to success and achieving your goals there are going to be tough times. There are going to be events that cause you to question the entire process and make you want to just give up right then and there. If you quit then you will never know what could have been.

I knew I would not be able to play, but I also knew that this team needed me as a part of their practice squad so they could get better. Although I wasn't able to help during games, I gave every single practice my all—I was not going to let this setback stop me. So I played on, for myself and for my team.

I came back every single day for practice and played like it was my last, because I knew that day was approaching rapidly. Every game day I had to re-live the consequences of my past mistakes. It was painful for me every week to watch our games, but I knew it was what was best for the team, so I did what I could. Every game I would dress to help the coaches and motivate the players to stay focused and keep their heads in the game.

While I was not a presence on the field, I made myself known on the sidelines. I felt that if I could not help my team physically I would help them emotionally and mentally. Every game I would come close to losing my voice from shouting encouragement from the sidelines.

The season came and went in what now seems like the blink of an eye. Our team had a record of 2-11 to finish the season. It was hard to watch because I knew I could have helped out tremendously, but couldn't because of the choices I had made in the past. It broke my heart.

At the end-of-the-season banquet dinner I was awarded the coaches award, despite my lack of playing time. My goal was to help as many other people succeed as possible and it showed when I was given that honor.

A few weeks later I was sitting at school eating my lunch and my football coach casually walked by and ask if I would like to play in the All-Star game. Without hesitation I responded with an excited "YEAH."

I never thought much of it after that because I figured it was such a long shot that I shouldn't get too emotionally attached to it. The All-Star Classic was a game I had watched every year since I started playing football. It is played at the same stadium the pros play in, and is a special event reserved for the best of the best high school players.

There are five divisions of high school football, 1–5, and they go by size of school. Typically the only players in the All-Star game are taken from division 1 and division 2 teams, the biggest and best-known teams in the county. The school I was in was in the 8-man football league. A division below division 5. It was for small schools with not enough draw and talent to put together a "true and traditional" football team. We took a lot of pride in our team, but at the same time we knew where we stood compared to some of the big schools.

I didn't know it at the time, but my coach had gone ahead and submitted me to the All-Star selectors because of my never-give-up approach and my work ethic throughout the season to help the team, even when I knew I wasn't going to play. The submission may have caught their attention because nobody from the 8-man league had even been submitted before, let alone selected.

About three months later I got an email while I was traveling on a school trip. I had been selected to play in the San Diego County All Star Classic. I couldn't believe what I was reading. I was on cloud nine. I would be able to put the pads back on again and play along some of San Diego's best players—players who were moving onto college teams in the fall.

I ran and told some of my old teammates and then immediately started training. That night I laced up the shoes and went for a run. It was time to get in shape to compete with the best of the best.

I spent the next two months training with my coach, one on one, to prepare for this game. I needed to bring myself up another level to even be competitive with these players. As I mentioned before, I had come a loooooong way in my journey to health and fitness, but this was going to require I take it to the next level. So we worked, day in and day out, every day. Then the day finally came for the first practice with the team.

I walked into the locker room that first day and was greeted and given looks that basically conveyed the message "who the heck is this guy and what is he doing here?" Most of the guys on the team did not even know that my school, the San Diego Jewish Academy, even existed. Some people made jokes, some people said nothing to me at all, but it didn't matter. I was there for one reason and one reason only—to play football, and that's what I did.

Not being the best on the field was not a new feeling for me, so I embraced it and did the only thing I could possibly do, give it my all every single chance that I got. My skill set was lacking compared to many of the other players, but what I lacked in skill I made up for in tenacity.

I volunteered to hit and get hit at every opportunity that came up. To the other players and coaches who doubted me in the beginning, one thing became very clear, I WOULD NOT QUIT.

Man, did I get rocked a few times. I took bigger hits than I had ever taken in my life. I probably inflicted more physical damage on myself in those three weeks of practice than I did my whole previous football career. I might have been a stud at the SDJA, but when you're lining up against guys who are going to D1 schools in the fall, your true colors show.

I was not given a starting position for the game, which wasn't totally surprising, but the coach did pull me aside one day and told me that they noticed how hard I was working. They knew the circumstances that brought me to that field, and said that I would absolutely see some game time. That's all I needed to hear.

Game day came and I put the pads on for the last time in my life. I felt surreal and honored to be a part of this tradition. The game started and I stayed on the sidelines, stuck to the hip of my defensive coordinator. I wanted him to know that when he needed someone to go in, I was ready. And late in the 4th quarter I got my chance. With about 5 minutes left to play I was put in as the left defensive end.

Chills went all through my body as I stepped on that field. I could hear my friends in the stands shouting, "Gilly, Gilly …!" It felt like everything had finally clicked into place and I was exactly where I was supposed to be. All my hard work throughout high school and especially the last few months had led up to this moment.

Five short plays later the whistle blew and that was the end of the game. My career had ended, but I felt fulfilled. I even had a half a tackle in the statistics.

The biggest lesson to take away from this experience is that in life we all fail, but it is about failing forward. To repeat: most people allow failure to be an answer, but it is merely a suggestion in the pursuit of something great in life. We must learn to fail forward to our success. Failure is merely a pit stop on the road to success, not the final destination.

"If at first you do not succeed, then you must try, try, try again."

Your road to success will not be easy, and you will have to pave it yourself. There will be times where you feel like giving up. Times when it seems like it makes sense to give up on what you want, but you must remind yourself of the bigger picture. The true purpose of a goal is not to achieve the goal, but to transform into the person you can become by pursuing it with everything you have got.

There is no greater loss in life than looking back and knowing you could have done better. Knowing that you allowed yourself to give up on your own goal. Anything is possible as long as you accept failure as part of the journey.

I wasn't going to allow my own failures to dictate my life. Nothing in life worth having is easy to get. You must learn to embrace failure as a part of the process if you want to achieve something great. The road to success is going to be bumpy and not what you expected, but if you are strong and embrace the failures, and use them to grow, you will be more successful than you ever thought you could be.

THE two things you can be CERTAIN OF: "Where you are is a result of who you were, but where you go depends entirely on who you choose to be."

> – Hal Elrod, International keynote speaker
> and NY Times best-selling author

"The moment you accept responsibility for everything in your life is the moment you gain the power to change anything in your life."

> – Hal Elrod, International keynote speaker
> and NY Times best-selling author

"Success consists of going from failure to failure without a loss of enthusiasm."

> -    Winston Churchill,  former Prime Minister of the UK
>
> -

"Never be afraid to fail, be afraid of not learning from your mistakes."

> - Unknown

"To make a decision means to cut off the other option. Once you have truly harnessed the power of a decision, the other option no longer exists."

> – Eric Gillman

So what choice are you ready to make today? Do you want to live your best life possible, or just settle on what's easy, settle for a life of mediocrity?

Robin Sharma once said, "One of the saddest things in life is to get to the end of your life and look back in regret, knowing that you could have been, done and had so much more."

We all have the desire to achieve; it is built into our brains. It is that warm feeling of pride when you get a test back with an A on it, or that gratifying feeling of winning the championship game. It's that yearning you feel when you know you could have done better, when you know you could have pushed yourself harder.

We all want to change the world somehow. Maybe you want to change the world through politics, maybe through business, maybe through acting, science, food, or engineering. It doesn't matter how you do it, but we all want something out of life. It's why we wake up in the morning and get out of bed.

The late, great rapper Notorious B.I.G. once said, "We can't change the world unless we change ourselves."

# CHAPTER 7
# 3 S.D.S. Key Areas for Life Mastery...It's SO DAMN SIMPLE!

I promised to tell you more about my running experience, going from a kid who couldn't finish one mile to, well, something more.

A friend of mine named Favian and I were roommates at a Miami work conference. This was over seven years after I told myself that I was not a runner. Favian is an accomplished distance racer, and has finished many marathons in his life. We sat outside on the patio discussing life, health and fitness. I shared with him that I appreciate what he does as a runner, but it simply was not for me.

As an accomplished runner, I'm sure my problems seemed a bit trivial to Favian, but he acknowledged them. He then suggested an idea to me that changed my life forever—one I hope could influence yours as well.

He explained to me that all of his accomplishments as an athlete were all built on failures that preceded them. I saw that not everything in life is going to go the way you want it. In fact, most of life is going to be discouraging and not the way that you intended it to be. But the world will not judge you by your failures; it will judge you by what you do to respond to them.

You must be willing to embrace failure as a step in the right direction. While it might not be as big of a step as you had planned on,

31

it is still a step in the right direction, and that is what it means to "fail forward towards success."

Knowing my running history, right there Favian placed a challenge in front of me that changed my life forever. Seeing that I had a deep admiration for his achievements, he suggested that I sign up to do a half-marathon, a 13.1-mile race.

In that moment I thought he was crazy, but then I took the first step that changed my life forever: I went on a three-mile run. That was something that previous to that moment, I would have told you was impossible. I will be the first to tell you—it was not pretty. Afterwards I was beat and felt exhausted, but at the same time I felt energized, renewed and invigorated.

So I started my training. One day at a time, putting left foot in front of the right and right foot in front of the left and I knew I was going to fail my way to the top, and that is exactly what happened. After five months of training I crossed the half-marathon finish line in just under two hours.

What is even more fulfilling than that moment is what that victory created afterwards. This spark allowed to me set a fire in my life: my passion for running and fitness, much of which led me to be writing this book today.

From my first half-marathon I went on to complete another, and then another, and then my first full marathon, then my first half-Ironman, and multiple small races in between. I also have been able to raise thousands of dollars for charity by having people sponsor my runs. I have had the opportunity to inspire many others to not be afraid of their own failure and to embrace something, some goal they might be afraid of. And it all started with one small choice: the choice to embrace failure as part of the process and fail forward towards your goal.

Our path to greatness is an ongoing process from which we fail forward to the goals we want to achieve in our lives. It's worth repeating: whether you realize it or not, we all are born with an innate sense to be great. It is born within us to strive to be better, to achieve higher, and in some way leave this world in better condition than when we entered into it.

Maybe you have lost touch with this sense, but it is there. It's that feeling of pride you get when you do something right, even if no one is looking or paying attention. It's the warm feeling you have in your heart when you are able to selflessly help someone else. It's the thoughts that run through your head when you hit the pillow at night, that little voice that tells you to do right over wrong, and strive to be the best version of yourself. And then be that person.

Everyone in this world is here for a reason, big or small. In order to best serve the world, we must live in pursuit of the best versions of ourselves.

**"Don't let the things that you can't do affect the things that you can do."**

**– Matthew Kelly, International keynote speaker and multiple best-selling author**

In my brief 27 years on this planet I have learned a thing or two about creating the best version of myself, so I may go onto help others by showing them how to do the same. **I believe that if in life you accomplish something that others find difficult, then you have a social responsibility to help the others around you. Many people believe the three greatest words spoken together are, "I DID IT." To accomplish a personal goal is truly an amazing feeling, but it is dwarfed in comparison to showing the next person how to do what you did, but to do it even better.**

I commonly get asked the question, "How did you do it?" or "What was the big thing that changed for you?" Both of these are great questions, and I am sure most people hope to hear some short answer about a diet I went on, or a book I read, or a seminar I attended, or a magic pill that I took that solved all my problems. The truth is, I mastered what I call the *S.D.S. keys for life mastery.*

What does S.D.S. stand for? I call these the three keys because they are "SO DAMN SIMPLE." Sometimes we spend large amounts of energy looking far and wide for answers that are two inches away from our nose. We hope for some magic solution to a simple problem that has been complicated by our own thoughts and excuses.

I have found that there are three key areas of your life that you must learn to take full control of, and by doing so, through making healthy choices, you will create the life of your dreams. Those three areas are: your health, your fitness and your wellness.

These three key areas will give you a holistic grasp of your entire life and put you back in the driver's seat. I will go into each of these in more detail, but to simply define the three areas: your health is what you put into your body, your fitness is what you output from your body, and your wellness is how you manage your thoughts and emotions in your body.

Let me share these simple keys with you so you have the tools needed to master any area of your own life. How would it feel to know you are in complete control of your life and your circumstances? How would it feel to look in the mirror and know the person looking back at you has exceeded your own expectations? What does the life of your dreams look like to you?

We can get there together and the very best part is; it's SO DAMN SIMPLE.

## 1. Your Health:

**"Let food be thy medicine."**

**– Hippocrates**

**"Take care of your body. It's the only place you have to live."**

**– Jim Rohn, International keynote speaker, author and motivational guru**

There are many different ways to define your health, but to keep this simple, let's classify your health as what you decide to put into your body. We all know the old saying, "You are what you eat," but how much do you believe that and how often does that guide your daily eating choices?

The human body is a magnificent machine. A highly efficient, highly tuned factory that can output incredible things. Look at some of the world's best athletes and see how finely tuned you can make your machine. Like any machine, the human body needs a high level of maintenance and specific fuels to keep it in peak state.

The problem with many people is that instead of treating their bodies like the finely tuned machines they could be, they treat them more like garbage disposals, putting just about anything in there because it's fast and easy.

Almost more important than what you eat is what you drink. As a culture we have steered away from nature's ultimate food. This is So Damn Simple, but overlooked by so many people in our world of never-ending options and choices.

**When it comes down to healthy things to drink there is only one answer: Water.** Water is the life source of the entire planet. It is what created us, it is what we are made of, and it is what we need in order to live at a peak state. You may know the human body consists of 70% water and it is in constant need of replenishment. Currently, the most widespread and common health problem in the world is not cancer, or the cold, but dehydration. Dehydration plagues more people than you know, in more ways than you could ever imagine, and most people don't even know it.

At this point you might be asking yourself some questions, like: how in such a modern society can so many people be dehydrated? Or, how can I be dehydrated—I drink all the time? For people seeing themselves as "drinking all the time," you have to consider what it is you're drinking and how it is affecting your body.

The main problem with this concept is that the majority of people are substituting all types of other stuff for water, mostly sodas and sugary juices, that don't actually contain any real juice, or nutritional value.

If you want to live at peak state, soda is the worst beverage to put into your body. What is soda? Think about it for a second. Most people would just say something like, "delicious, or bubbly."

But let's take a step back here and take a look at soda from an objective point of view. Say we were aliens who just came to planet earth to observe and study how its people live. We would see highly advanced human beings that have created an amazingly in-depth and functional society. This was accomplished through innovation and the use of our logic. Now consider we, the aliens, looked at what people consume to replenish their bodies. Considering that humans are made up of 70% water, anyone, alien or not, would assume that this brilliant logic would guide us to always, or at least most of the time, drink water, and nothing else.

However, the reality is that you would observe humans consuming bubbly drinks that come in neatly decorated plastic bottles. The contents of these bottles are listed on the side, but the people drinking them have absolutely no idea what these chemicals are, let alone how to pronounce most of them.

When I was really heavy, I drank a lot of diet soda, at least two liters a day. I thought I needed it in my life, but the truth was quite the opposite.

Let me be clear to you: you absolutely can change this habit. It is so ridiculously simple and easy. You just have to make the decision to do what's right, not what's easy. Water is available in every single place that soda is sold, everywhere, and even better, it's usually available for free. We, as a culture, choose the soda because it feels and tastes good and keeping that habit is easier than making a healthy change of routine to drinking water.

Here is another cool fact that will change your life. The majority of the time that you think you are hungry, you are actually just dehydrated. WHAT? The first thing your body does when it is dehydrated is it sends a message to your brain to replenish. However, your mind doesn't process it quite right and you think you are hungry. And what do we do when we are hungry? We eat ... oh yeah we do.

But here is the ridiculously simple thing you can do. The next time you feel really hungry or some kind of craving coming on, drink two glasses of water. Just do it, simple enough. Wait ten minutes and see if you're still hungry. Don't believe me; try it yourself next time you "have to eat."

Here is the big secret of how I lost 17 pounds in 4 months. Here is the "big change" I made that I think people want to know about. **I switched from drinking a 20-ounce diet soda to drinking a 1.5-liter bottle of water every day before lunch. THAT'S IT! No big crazy complicated secret. One simple change from what's easy to what's right. And what's clearly better.**

Many people are shocked to learn that the remedy was something that simple, but it truly *is* that easy. Will drinking only water turn your whole life around? Probably not, but it is a step in the process of creating your best self, the self that can create the life of your dreams, and thereby help others as well.

**If you want long lasting change in your own life, it starts by making small changes every single day. Small changes every day are the foundation to building your healthy and successful future. It is commonly thought that you need to make drastic change in all areas of your life to deeply change, but that is not sustainable. People can't last like that, and the habits will eventually break and go back to the way they were before, or worse.**

**In order to have lasting change you must be willing to make small, but permanent, changes in your life every day.**

I propose a water challenge to you. For the next 30 days drink ONLY water. That's right, nothing else but water: no soda, no coffee, no energy drinks, no juices, just water. I bet you notice a difference in the first few days and continued success from that point onwards.

Is it worth it to you to make a minor change that will have a massive effect on your life? Will it be difficult at first? Probably, but remember, **nothing worth having is easy to get.** Keep this in mind when challenging yourself to something for 30 days. The first 10 days will be unbearable, the second 10 days will be uncomfortable, and the last 10 days you will be unstoppable. Allow your body to be cleansed by the one thing it truly needs the most, water.

## MAKE FOOD FOR FUNCTION NOT JUST FUN.

What you decide to eat can be a bit more complex. There are so many more options for food than drink and so many opportunities to make unhealthy choices. There are thousands of books written on health and food and I encourage you to do more research for yourself into *what your body needs,* because we are all truly different.

I am not a registered dietitian or nutritionist, but I am someone who has experimented with many methods for myself and others and I am eager to share the knowledge I have acquired along the way. Every person has a different metabolism and digestive system, so I encourage you to find what is the best recipe for your success. But I want to share the most simplified and uncomplicated ways to determine what you eat. It's So Damn Simple.

To keep this simple and easy for everyone to apply immediately, we are going to classify foods into two basic categories: Live food versus dead food. Live food is not a particular food itself, but foods that contain a high content of water in them and are thereby living foods. These living foods are what your body needs on a regular basis. The simplest foods that are live and contain high amounts of water are your fruits and vegetables, raw and uncooked.

Some examples of these high water-content fruits include many favorites: strawberries, grapefruit, blueberries, apples and pears. All of these are delicious and best of all they require no time to prep or cut— you just eat them. These fruits all have water content of over 70% per volume, which is approximately how much of the human body consists of water. Some of the best vegetables with the highest water content include: lettuce, tomatoes, cucumbers, broccoli, peppers or spinach. Again, all of these vital foods can be eaten raw, or prepared in an endless amount of ways. These simple plant-based foods will allow your body to process all the nutrients and water that is in the food and allow your body to use it most efficiently.

We will become what we eat. Don't believe me? Go sit in a McDonald's for an hour and observe the people coming and going. Then go to your local healthy supermarket or farmers market and observe the people who shop there. What do they look like to you? What version of yourself would you rather strive to be?

Remember this simple guideline and it will steer you in the right directions: **food for function, not fun.** As a culture we use food as entertainment and celebration, not as an essential building block for who we want to become. Food can be fun. Trust me, there are sooooo many healthy—and tasty—options and restaurants where you can eat; you just have to be willing to do what's right, not what's easy.

Contrast live foods with what I call dead foods. These should be avoided at all costs and be cut out of a diet as much as possible. These are foods that your body has virtually no use for, or will have trouble processing. Like many things in life, all these foods measure on a spectrum from vital nutrients to unnecessary processed junk.

Dead foods include foods that are processed. A simple way to understand what a processed food is, is to look at it and ask: is this food in its natural state?

I'm not saying that you need to cut all these things out of your diet *completely,* because drastic change to diet is not lasting. However, it is wise to be aware of the main food groups that do not contribute to a healthier you. You must find a balance in your life that works for you and keep practicing it every day.

**The best foods are the ones that do not have nutrition labels on them.**

They are not measured in calories, fat content or carbs. They are measured by ripeness, size and taste. Do not judge a food by artificial ingredients that are not made for your body, but look to things that help your body function.

So that's it! Drink only water and eat live foods. My revolutionary eating habits might shock you. The truth is that you already know what's right, but you just have to make the conscious decision to do what's right—not what's easy.

## THREE TIPS FOR EATING HEALTHY EVERY DAY

**1. Pack your own food every day:** Commonly, the reason people make unhealthy choices when it comes to food is because they feel what's available is their only option. Give yourself the ability to make a healthy choice by packing your own lunch every day. You control your own life and choices, so act accordingly and feel the difference. You can use a simple cooler or even a plastic grocery bag if you cannot afford a cooler. My recommendation is the "6-pack food management system." Check it out online. It's basically the Rolls Royce of lunch boxes and it's very affordable. There are several different options out there, in all different price ranges, so find the one that works best for you. Make your cooler a permanent sidecar to your life.

**2. Never go anywhere without your water:** Dehydration leads to hunger, which leads to unhealthy eating. Most of us live in a world where water is readily available and usually free. This is a privilege I think many people take for granted; I encourage you to not. Invest in a reusable water bottle that can go anywhere with you. I recommend the Hydro Flask, which keeps drinks cold or hot for hours on end, but any water bottle will do. The point is to not let yourself fall into dehydration.

The normal recommendation for fluid consumption a day is 6–8 glasses, including water and anything else you drink. Even if you follow my recommendation and drink only water, personally I believe this is way too little. From my own experience and the experiences of others **you should be consuming half your weight in pounds, in ounces of water a day.** That means if you weigh 130 pounds you should be drinking approximately 65 fluid ounces of water a day. If you weigh 250 pounds you should shoot to consume 125 ounces of water a day. This might seem like a lot to some people, but by simply switching out other drinks for water this number is much more achievable. Just a word of caution: it is actually possible to get sick from drinking too much water, through over-diluting the nutrients in your body, so don't bloat yourself by drinking way more than these approximate targets. You're aiming to make your body efficient, not turn yourself into a human water-balloon. Find an amount of water that keeps your body comfortably hydrated every day and stick to it.

**3. Plan to fail forward:** As we already learned, failure is a part of the process of creating the best version of yourself. This is no different when it comes to what you eat. You must learn to enjoy your diet around your life and not your life around your diet. I don't even like the word "diet" because frankly, "diets" don't work. They are temporary and focus on cutting out certain foods completely and restricting the natural urge to enjoy life. They are usually for a certain amount of time and a certain goal, like lose thirty pounds in thirty days, or drop carbs for two months to drop weight. While these might have temporary results, they usually fail miserably in the long run.

There will be things that come up in your life that make you want to deviate from your normal healthy eating habits. No matter how much you try to escape it, food is tied into our culture and lives. Family BBQs, weddings, birthdays, office parties, and most social gatherings revolve around food. My suggestion is not to completely cut yourself out of these events, or withdraw from eating a piece of cake on your birthday. Life is too short to withhold completely from life's little pleasures. However, all too often we use these occasions to completely let go of our inhibitions and thereby we sacrifice days or weeks of hard work.

My suggestion is to set a specific goal for yourself for a specific thing you want badly. Don't go with a loose expectation such as: if I eat healthy Monday-Saturday, I will eat whatever I want on Sunday. Trust me, you can easily undo six days of healthy eating habits with one day of limitless inhibition.

Have a specific reward in mind and allow yourself to enjoy life's little pleasures, but don't live for them. Let me give you an example. I LOVE macaroni and cheese. It is my favorite food and I would eat it all day every day if I could, but unfortunately that's not a realistic way to live, unless I wanted to weigh 500 pounds. Growing up, because it was my favorite, every year for my birthday we would have mac and cheese.

It has a special place in my heart, but not my gut. A way you can live a fulfilling life and use healthy choices to lead it is to plan to fail forward. I am not saying I only eat mac and cheese once a year, but one time that I absolutely do is the "Macaroni and Cheese Festival." That's right, you heard that right. Knowing that something like this is coming up I always plan to fail forward. Do I not indulge at the festival.... HELL NO!

However, I do plan a few weeks ahead to do just a bit extra during my workout. Leading up to the event I will add an additional two miles onto whatever cardio I am planning on doing that day. It's not a ton, but it adds up and fills my commitment account. This way when the festival rolls around, and it's time to chow down, I can do so knowing that I have already planned to fail forward.

The point is you must allow yourself to fail forward to your success of healthy eating. Sometimes it will be an up-and-down journey, but you must remind yourself to stay on the road to success, and not pull over for fast food.

## ACTION STEPS

- 30-day water challenge
- prepare your own food every day
- never go anywhere without some of your own healthy food and water
- fail forward towards your goal

## 2. Your Fitness:

I would bet everyone reading this has attempted some fitness goal in the past and failed, and that is totally okay. But remember this: "If you want to love your body you must make it a healthy body." Let me be very clear, I did not say skinny or thin body, I said *healthy*. **Your goal shouldn't be to look a certain way, as much as it should be to *feel* a certain way.**

That way should be: to feel happy and confident in your own body, whatever that means to you. A healthy body is not a skinny body. Look at me; I am by no means a skinny person, but I am healthy and I know that's how I feel—that's what is important.

So the only true way to make your body healthy is through fitness. Your body is made to move, it wants to move, so give it what it wants. We are enmeshed in sedentary lifestyles. We drive everywhere, sit all day and have food delivered to us whenever we request it. This is not the way the human body was designed to function.

If you go back in history, only 200–300 years ago, people had to search for their food. They had to go out and hunt, fish or farm every day in order to obtain their food. This exerted a lot of energy. We also walked or ran everywhere. Nowadays you would be hard pressed to find someone who would voluntarily walk a mile to the store instead of drive.

Since this is the life we have settled into, it is imperative that we adjust our lifestyles to compensate for this lack of movement. I can't tell you exactly what to do, but I can and will tell you that in order to succeed at the three key areas of making healthy choices you MUST make fitness a part of your life and who you are.

For many of us we quit on ourselves far too easily and coin ourselves as "not able to exercise," for whatever reason. We give up on the battle before even stepping foot on the battleground. This is no way to live your life. You are an extraordinary being, capable of incredible things. I know this because years ago I was the guy who threw in the towel before the fight even started.

Remember this concept when it comes to fitness: **"Every day a little bit faster, a little bit stronger, a little bit better, every day."** Fitness is a long and never-ending road. While that might sound daunting, it shouldn't be. This road is filled with constant improvement. Constantly proving to yourself that you are capable of being better. Every day you have the ability to create a stronger, faster and better version of yourself.

When I couldn't even finish running one mile in 6th grade it killed my self-esteem. I thought it was impossible to run, let alone a whole mile. This thought became my reality, and I basically gave up on running, and most physical activity. I remember thinking to myself: "It's impossible for me to run a mile, so why even try."

This type of thinking serves no one, especially yourself. If you give up on something before you ever even try it, you are robbing yourself of the person you could be. That could have been it for me. I thought it was impossible for me to run a mile, let alone in a respectable time.

That is all *impossible* is; something that people have not seen done yet. It is a label that people like to throw around to shield them from having to attempt to do something difficult. As humans, we are programmed to find the path of least resistance, a topic we will cover more later.

As far back as human history goes people have been doing things that others thought were impossible. Centuries ago people thought it was impossible to build a building that could touch the sky, but now we have buildings that tower over 100 stories. Decades ago we thought it was impossible to send messages via linked computers, but now the Internet connects the entire world in just seconds. And years ago we thought it was impossible to have a device that could make calls, track locations, send messages, take pictures and much more, yet now most people have iPhones, Droids, or access to other smartphones.

The point is that impossible is not truly "Impossible," just something people have not seen yet. The very word itself says, "I'M POSSIBLE."

## BREAK THROUGH YOUR OWN IMPOSSIBLE BARRIERS

Let me share with you a quick story to prove that impossible is not only nothing, but merely a jumping-off point for all the amazing things the future holds. In 1954 Roger Bannister became the first person to run a full mile in under four minutes; he must have been taking notes from my mile. Just kidding.

Previous to this event, it was commonly believed that it was impossible for a human to run a mile in under four minutes. This belief stood for centuries until one day in June of 1954 Roger Bannister did the impossible and ran the mile in 3:58.

That event is remarkable, but what is truly amazing about this is not the event itself, but what proceeded to happen after he ran the mile. This "impossible" record that stood for practically all time was beaten a mere nine months later, when someone else ran it in 3:49. [And beaten again not long after that]

The point is that once people see that impossible is nothing it becomes only a word. IMPOSSIBLE IS A SUGGESTION NOT AN ANSWER. If you can see yourself complete something, then this impossible task is something you can work towards.

To be able to see yourself complete a task and visualize the success is one of the most vital tools we will cover later in this book.

Visualization of goals is not a secret, and it has been used by some of the world's most successful people. When you close your eyes and think about that goal you want to achieve you must see yourself as the person who has achieved it and then work towards being that person every day. If your goal is to be an excellent runner, maybe even run a marathon, then visualize that person every day and then make the choices that that person would make every day and you will slowly but surely see yourself become the person who you visualized before.

Maybe your goal is just to be able to walk a certain distance without feeling fatigued, or play with your kids without having to take a break. See that person and take steps towards becoming that person everyday by making choices that THAT PERSON would make.

Jim Carrey, one of the world's best-known actors and comedians wrote himself a check for $10,000,000 in 1984 for "acting services rendered." He visualized that goal and worked towards it for years. It was almost exactly 10 years later on Christmas of 1994 when he received a check for $10 million for his role in *Dumb and Dumber*. Do you think at some point Jim Carrey thought it was impossible to make $10 million for acting? Of course he had his doubts, but once he could visualize it, it was no longer impossible.

Visualization is a key component of success in any area of life, not just fitness. Some of the world's greatest actors visualize themselves as the people they are portraying on screen or stage and the result is some of the best performances we have ever known.

See yourself as the person you want to become and act as if that person would until you turn yourself into that person.

## ACTION STEPS:

- Visualize yourself achieving your goal, no matter how big or small

- Don't let personal or mental barriers stop you from pursuing it

## MY "IMPOSSIBLE MILE"

As an obese 12-year-old, I thought it was impossible to run a mile without dying. Since we're talking about how to achieve fitness, let's go back to that life-changing conversation with my friend Favian, already an accomplished marathon and endurance runner.

As I said, Favian and I worked together at the time and we roomed together at a conference we were both attending in Miami. One beautiful Florida evening we were sitting outside of a hotel room on the patio talking about life, health and fitness.

I shared with him that I couldn't do more than a mile or two without some major discomfort. I told him my story of my epic 14-minute mile and said that running simply 'wasn't my thing.'

He acknowledged this, but then asked me if I had even tried running a mile since then. I told him that I had done it from time to time, but never really pushed myself past that point. I told him that 2 miles was my limit and I could not make it past that.

He then asked me a question I will never forget. He said; "Eric, how would you know your limits until you push yourself to them."

I thought, "Huh, I never thought of it that way."

Favian then suggested that I sign up for a half-marathon, 13.1 miles. My first thought was, *no way,* but after letting the idea stew around for a while I thought to myself: Why not? You miss 100% of the shots you never take.

With Favian's encouragement, and the natural urge to live a healthy life, I signed up to do my first half-marathon. I had no idea what I was doing to get ready, or even if I had a chance to complete it.

So I started at the only place we can all start a massive journey in life: the beginning. One day at a time I started running a bit more and more. Every day I felt myself getting a little bit stronger and a little bit faster. I even started to repeat this in my head while I was running. "Every day a little bit stronger, every day a little bit faster."

People want drastic change in their lives, in all different ways, but success cannot come overnight. Although sometimes, from an outside perspective, it might seem like change in someone's life happened quickly or drastically, in reality it is the culmination of hundreds or thousands of small decisions that led him or her to that moment of triumph.

The small changes you make every day in your life will become the drastic change that others cannot see develop from the outside.

So I kept running, every day a little bit faster, every day a little bit stronger, every day. One foot in front of the other, one mile at a time. Started with 2 miles, then 5, then 7, until the race day finally came and went. I finished the half-marathon, but it left me hungry for growth. I went on to complete a full marathon, 26.2 miles, about a year after that. After that was done, I continued to stay hungry for growth. I then signed up and completed my first half-IRONMAN. For those of you not familiar with that race, it is a 1.5-mile swim, 56-mile bike ride, and a 13.1-mile run, totaling 70.3 miles. It took me just over 6 hours.

If you had run into me 10 years earlier, the day after I had been marked "Not Able," for my 6th-grade mile, and told me that in 10 years I would go on to complete a marathon, I would think you were crazy and giving the message to the wrong person. I would have told you it was absolutely impossible! That young version of me did not know yet that impossible was simply something we have not seen done yet. People have been doing the impossible for centuries, even millennia, and that is what makes the world great.

The key to remember is that impossible is nothing, and it all starts with your very first step. Do not focus on the long journey that may lie ahead of you, but instead just focus your energy on the next step you have to take, AND TAKE IT. There is nothing between you and your goals except you. Take the first step today towards your goals, the next one tomorrow, and never stop until you get there.

## 5 ways to start getting fit RIGHT NOW!

When it comes to fitness just remember this and repeat it to yourself every time you work out: "Every day a little bit faster, a little bit stronger, a little bit better, every day."

How do you get to running 5, 10, 25 miles: start with 1. Can't run it, walk it. Then the next day, walk it a bit faster, and the next week jog it and just keep growing yourself in a positive direction.

Here are five easy ways to get immediately moving toward a fit lifestyle. One of the five of these usually works for any situation.

1. Join a team; if in school, an after-school sports program, youth league, adult league, free fitness groups or local sports program.

2. Join a gym and go to all the free classes

If you can afford a personal trainer get one, but if you can't afford it, just ask someone. Just walk up to someone in the gym and ask if they could give you 1–2 exercises to improve your ____. Do this a few times to different people and before you know it, you're trained. A little secret you might not know about very healthy people—they are generally in a good mood and willing to help those willing to learn.

3. Get a workout buddy. Hopefully enlist a friend who is willing to train you, or just another plus-sized warrior like yourself, on a mission to live a healthier lifestyle.

4. Get off your booty and go outside. Outside is filled with endless activities. Play sports with friends; get games started. If you can't find anyone, then do it yourself: run, bike, swim, basketball, anything. Absorb the energy of the sun and let it fuel your thirst for personal growth.

5. IF YOU CAN'T SEEM TO FIND THE RESOURCES TO DO ANY OF THOSE THINGS:

Just get outside and start walking. Start moving yourself in the direction of living a healthier lifestyle. You don't even have to run to start off. Do what you're comfortable with now, and then push yourself a bit further every day.

Walk instead of drive, take the stairs every time instead of the escalator, stretch every morning for five minutes and allow blood to start flowing through you. The possibilities are endless; just start doing something that will move you closer to the person you desire to be.

## 3. Your Wellness: How you manage your thoughts and emotions

### THE POWER OF VISUALIZATION AND EXPECTATION: Find your why

We all want something out of life, and that something is different for every person. Deep within us is unlimited potential, and life is all about finding out the true reason why we were put on this Earth and pursuing that potential like there is no other option. Make your own decisions on what you want out of life and "cut off" the option of not achieving them. In order to fulfill our goals and dreams we must first set a goal, break it down to what it takes to accomplish and work towards creating that version of ourselves every single day. We also must not be afraid to fail forward to our goals.

Let's start with something simple. What is something you want to achieve out of your life, or out of reading this book? When you listen to that voice inside of your mind, what is it yearning for? Humans are amazing creatures that are capable of incredible things, and you are no different. Within each and every one of us is something special. In some way, shape or form we all have gifts others don't. Your mission in life should be to find what really drives you and use it to propel you to be the successful person you want to become.

I WANT TO ACCOMPLISH _____ IN MY LIFE!

What is something you want to accomplish in the next year? More importantly what would it mean for you to achieve this goal? It is important to not only have goals, but also have a *why* that drives them. The goal is a vehicle, but the why is the fuel that will drive you there. A goal without a why will get you nowhere, fast.

TO ACCOMPLISH _____WOULD MEAN
_____

In order to start the process of failing forward we have to set something to fail forward to. Think about it, and don't be afraid to think big. What do you want out of life? Maybe it is something big like change the world through politics, maybe it is something as simple as living a healthy life with a good family. Think about it and allow that vision to become a part of who you are. What is something you want, and more importantly, why do you want it? What does it mean to you to achieve it? The why is what will keep you up late at night thinking about it, and it will drive you to get out of bed in the morning. A goal without a strong why is not very useful at all. It is simple to say that you are going for something big, but if you don't have a strong why, then you will not have the resolve to stay committed to it.

Now you must create urgency behind this goal and set a time in which you would want to accomplish it. **Goals are just dreams with deadlines!**

When do you want to accomplish this goal? In an ideal world, when will it be something that you have accomplished? Put a date on it and start to move yourself in that direction every day! Small change every day is what will make long-lasting change in your life.

I WILL ACCOMPLISH _____ BY
_____!

Whether or not you actually hit your goal by this date is somewhat irrelevant. If you don't set a date in which you want to hit a goal it will never get done. It will sit in the back of your mind and stay there until you create urgency in your own life by putting a specific date to it. If you accomplish the goal by the goal date, that is awesome and you should be very proud of your accomplishment. But if you don't accomplish it by the date, it is all part of the process of failing forward. Embrace the process and know that even though you didn't hit exactly what you wanted by a certain date, you are much further ahead than you would have ever been if you hadn't set the goal date. Fail forwards to the person you want to become.

**"Dedication means staying committed to a goal, long after the initial motivation has worn off."** It is easy for someone to just throw something out there, but until you give it a meaning, it will never serve you or allow you to create the life that you truly want.

"I will not make excuses for the person I know I can be and I will make constant progress towards the goals I want to achieve."

# CHAPTER 8
# The 5 Pillars of Creating the Life of Your Dreams through Making Healthy Choices

"What some folks call impossible, is just stuff they haven't seen before."

*– What Dreams May Come*

"The moment you tell yourself you "Can't" do something, is the moment you rob yourself of the divine feeling it is to achieve something."

*– Eric Gillman*

What is something in your life that you would like to accomplish, but to achieve it seems impossible? What is your biggest, scariest goal, that when you think about it you become afraid to even pursue it?

## 1. LOOK TO THE TOP OF THE MOUNTAIN, THEN FOCUS ON YOUR NEXT STEP FORWARD:

"If you always put limits on everything you do, physical or anything else, it will spread into your work and into your life. There are no limits. There are only plateaus; and you must not stay there, you must go beyond them."

*– Bruce Lee*

**"What is the best way to eat an elephant? One bite at a time"**

**– Unknown**

The small changes every day will be the massive change you want from your life.

In life we all want big things: to graduate from college, to run a marathon, to get a certain job, to raise a family, to help others through charity, or maybe own our own company. When we think about our goals, sometimes they are so big it is difficult to wrap our head around achieving them.

We declare we want something, then that little voice of doubt comes along and says, "It's too big," or "How are you ever going to do that?" It is in our human nature to doubt ourselves when we set our goals toward something high. It is like a defense mechanism that your body has in place to protect itself from failure.

When a mountain climber declares he is going to climb Mt. Everest, he or she will first look to the top of the mountain to see where they want to eventually end up—but then the important thing is to focus on the very next step forward.

Sometimes we get caught up in the massive journey that is the top, and we fail to realize that a massive goal is achieved one small step at a time, not in giant bounds to the top. We must know what we want; that will keep us driven, but then only focus on the very next step to get you there. Small changes and movements every day is what will become the massive change you seek out of your life.

When I am embarking on a run of over 20 miles, or a bike ride of over 100 miles, I first ask myself: where do I want to end up? That is an exciting place, but it is key that from then on out I just focus on taking my next step, and my next step and my next step, because that is what will get me there.

Look towards the top of the mountain and know where you want to end up, then look down at the ground right in front of you and focus on just the very next step, just that one step forward. Break it down to the ridiculous and move towards it slowly but surely every day. When a climber is going to embark on climbing Mt. Everest they start at the base camp, looking at the peak of the mountain. Then they make a plan and take it one step at a time.

What is a goal in your life that is so big it scares you, but you know you can achieve it? What is your mountaintop? Now ask yourself, what can I do TODAY, right now to get there? What is my next step? How can I ensure I take one step in a positive direction toward what I want to achieve in my life? Write it down.

MY BIGGEST GOAL IS

_____

MY NEXT STEP TOWARDS MY GOAL **TODAY** IS

_____

## SUMMARY AND WORK PAGE:

* I WANT TO ACCOMPLISH _____ IN MY LIFE!

* TO ACCOMPLISH _____ WOULD MEAN
_____

* MY BIGGEST GOAL IS
_____

* MY NEXT STEP TOWARDS MY GOAL **TODAY** IS_____

* I WILL ACCOMPLISH _____ BY
_____!

Once you have filled in the spaces above I want you to copy this page out of the book (or print it if you're reading a digital copy) and make as many copies of it as possible. Post these up in as many places as you can as a constant reminder of the goals you want to achieve and the person you wish to become.

If you ever need more blank copies of this page you can find them on my website, EricGillman.com. Print them out, fill them out and put them everywhere as a constant reminder of the person you want to become.

Repeat these goals and visions to yourself every day and remind yourself of the life you are going to create for yourself through making healthy choices. Look to the mountaintop every day, and then plant your next step forward towards success. Some people might think it is silly to have these reminders all over the place, but these are the same people who will make excuses for their own lives and not achieve their goals. On your road to success there will be people who doubt you and think what you are doing is stupid or unnecessary, but that's not important. What is important is that you are doing what makes you happy and improves your life.

**The moment we take responsibility for everything in our own lives is the moment we can change anything in our lives.**

## DO WHAT'S RIGHT, NOT WHAT'S EASY

**"Nothing worth having is easy to get"**

**– Eric Gillman**

**"There's no traffic on the extra mile"**

**– Rickey Minor, International Music Director**

In our day-to-day lives we are always faced with thousands of choices. In most cases there is usually a choice that seems to be the easier of the two, but the catch is that the easy choice is very rarely the right choice. In our society, we are conditioned to take the path of least resistance to get to our goals.

This is the invisible trap that so many people fall into while pursuing their goals. We are born with this urge to find the easiest way out of situations. In today's culture of instant gratification and quick results, it is difficult to stand your ground and knowingly pick the more difficult thing to do.

To succeed at anything in life you must understand and embrace the fact that the right thing to do in your life is commonly not the easy thing to do. Think about it. We all know the right thing to do is eat a healthy diet and exercise. But how many times do pizza and Netflix win the battle over your free time? Or how about this—we all know the right thing to do is get to school or work prepared and on time, but so many times the snooze button convinces us otherwise.

To understand this further let's look into why we generally pick the easy things over the right things.

It comes down to the difference between choosing pleasure over happiness. While these two words might seem the same to some people, they are actually very different. For this book's purpose, pleasure is defined as: "something that brings you joy only as long as the activity sustaining it continues." What that means is that whenever the activity producing the pleasure ceases, so does the feeling of satisfaction that comes with it.

The most common pleasure-seeking activity that we all take part in is eating. Eating is a complete pleasure activity, especially when indulging in rich foods. We have all chowed down on a huge meal that was delicious, but soon after finishing that decadent meal we lose the sensation we were feeling while we were eating it. Sometimes this feeling is even accompanied by regret, because we know that gorging was not the right thing to do.

Maybe you know it was the wrong decision, but you do it anyways and even want to stop halfway through. I know I have been chowin' down on some burgers before, and mid-burger, thought consciously that this was probably not best for me, but then made the decision to power through anyways. Sound familiar at all?

Other pleasure-seeking activities include watching TV, playing video games, doing drugs and other substances and sexual experiences. These are all things that might "feel good" while doing them, but they do not provide any sustainable joy and well-being in your life. In fact, by indulging in too much pleasure-seeking activity we desensitize ourselves to it and constantly are in need of more.

Happiness, on the other hand, is quite different than pleasure. Activities that provide happiness will be defined as: "activities where joy continues to manifest itself, after the activity producing it has ceased."

Happiness is lasting and can create massive change in one's life. We all want to be happy in life, but we end up sacrificing this happiness in the pursuit of pleasure. Some examples of activities that produce happiness are working out, reading, learning or personal development. We have all had days where we didn't feel like doing something active, but we convinced ourselves to do it anyway because it was something we were committed to. Activities that produce happiness are like investing in yourself and growing yourself as a person.

Other things that will provide a large level of happiness include studying and developing yourself mentally and physically. These are things that provide pleasure after you stop doing them. Think about it; you study 50 hours for a big exam, you stop studying, you take the exam and you get an A. That feeling of pleasure came from hard work done weeks ago and it will continue for a long time. Maybe that A is what gets you into college or law school—how much pleasure and happiness would come from that? And even further, how much pleasure could you have because you made the healthy choice so many years ago that is still providing pleasure in your life?

People are all pleasure-seeking creatures. Unfortunately, it is something that is built into our brains. We are made to seek pleasure through food and sex because those are the two biological imperatives to continue life. These two options were simpler thousands of years ago before we lived in a culture that is over-saturated with pleasurable activities.

If you want to see how much of a pleasure-seeking society we are, walk down the street in most any city in the United States. Almost every other business has something to do with pleasure-seeking activity, not happiness. Fast food chains, convenience stores, liquor stores, and places that sell lottery tickets are virtually everywhere you look. They promise you temporary pleasure in exchange for money, but give you nothing sustainable after that.

It is critical that we be aware of the distinction between these two: pleasure and happiness. In order to live the life of our dreams by making healthy choices we must stay clear on this distinction, and constantly remind ourselves to invest time in activities that will give us long-term happiness and continue to do so long after the activity has ceased.

## 2. THE TRUE PURPOSE OF A GOAL

We all have goals in life, whether they are deliberate or subconscious. We have subconscious goals such as to get through the day without getting hit by a bus, and deliberate goals such as passing a class, or losing some weight. Goals are different for everyone and I can't tell you what to choose as your goal.

Goals can be big and scary sometimes and we fear to pursue them because they are too overwhelming. Goals can also be so small and insignificant that we ignore them because we don't feel they are truly important. Whatever the goal in your life, is it important to realize the true purpose of setting a goal. One concept that is very important to grasp is about setting and pursuing goals. The true purpose of setting and pursuing a goal is not necessarily to hit the goal itself, but **to grow as a person in the pursuit of the goal.** As I mentioned before, a goal is a dream with a deadline. By pursuing a goal we are forced to grow into a better person. The true reward of achieving a goal is not the reward itself, but the person you have become while going for the goal.

Take for example the college graduate. When they go to their graduation, walk across the stage and pick up the diploma it could be one the highlights of their life. As they reflect later that day, looking at their diploma, it serves as a symbol; a symbol of the person they have become. It is a symbol of the thousands of positive choices and changes they made in order to achieve it.

The true value of setting goals is not always necessarily the great feeling of hitting the goal itself. The true value comes from being the person who makes hundreds of healthy choices in pursuit of something bigger. You become the type of person who is willing to sacrifice and fight for something you want. You become this person by making one decision at a time.

For example, your goal is to lose 20 pounds in the next 3 months. Let's say you only lost 18 pounds and did not hit your original goal. There is a silver lining in this failure, because although you did not hit your original goal of 20, you still grew as a person, one who in order to lose the 18 pounds made hundreds of good choices over bad choices. On many occasions you made the right decision to eat the fruits and vegetables instead of the fats and carbs.

When you set a goal to do something and make an effort to reach it, then you are training your brain that you are capable of making the right decisions. Every time you make a decision that is the right choice, not the easy choice, you condition your brain to continue to make these choices. The human brain is in some ways no different than any other muscle in the body. It can be strengthened and conditioned, but it needs to be worked on like any other muscle in the body. Every good decision you make strengthens the fibers in the brain to make that decision again. The first time is always difficult, but as you strengthen it will get easier with time.

The process of pursuing these goals continues to condition the brain to always do what's right, not what is easy. By building this muscle in the brain, you make future goals and decisions easier than before because you know to do what's right, not what's easy.

## 3. HYPER AWARENESS

**"Is what I am doing right now moving me closer to or further away from my goal?"**

A simple question that we rarely stop and ask ourselves in our day-to-day lives. We get so caught up on autopilot on the ride of life that we rarely stop and recognize what we are doing.

Have you ever been there before? You set a goal to get a high grade on an assignment, but then find yourself on the back end of a Netflix marathon or a Facebook binging session. Looking at yourself in the reflection of your screen, wondering: "What just happened? Where did the time go?"

In order to survive in life we are all taught to be aware of our surroundings. This is a survival instinct we have from birth. Don't walk too close to the edge of a cliff, don't poke a poisonous snake, don't touch the fire. These are all things that anyone and everyone should be aware of to make it through life.

The problem for so many of us is that your state of awareness stops there. It only caters to your most basic survival and pleasure-seeking needs, which are basically to make it to the next day without falling off a cliff or into a fire. However, in order to thrive in life you must exercise a higher level of awareness, a level that will propel you to the next step in your own life. This is what I call **Hyperawareness.**

Hyperawareness is a heightened state of awareness that allows us to be present in almost every situation and realign ourselves with what it is we truly want.

In our day-to-day lives we all are guilty of getting caught drifting away from the conscious activities that align with our goals and desires. We can know that something is not good for us or our goals, but despite that we tell that little voice in our head to take a hike and we do it anyways.

Unfortunately, consistent awareness is something that can be easily overcome by deterrents and distractions. We can be knowingly aware that something is not good for us or that takes us from what we want to achieve, but we choose to speak over that voice and follow through with the action anyway.

For example, let's say you have set a goal to lose 10 pounds in the next 5 weeks. If this is your goal you are aware of it most of the time, but when it is time to go to a friend's BBQ party, awareness might not be enough by itself. You are aware of the goal, but you make the conscious choice to ignore this awareness and let go a bit on your original goal.

Another example would be if you have to get an assignment done by a certain date, but the night you are about to sit down and do it a friend of yours calls to hang out. Although you are aware of what you were supposed to do, your actions might speak otherwise, and you might not follow through on what you said you were going to do. The point is, everyone has a sense of awareness; it is built into us as human beings, but awareness is something that can be overcome by a lack of integrity and vision. This is why in order to achieve your goals, you must exercise a state of HYPERAWARENESS.

Hyperawareness is a state that supersedes a regular state of awareness. It is a necessary element in order to stay on track to hit any goal you desire in life. Without this vital tool we are destined to continue to fall off track of what we really want to achieve each and every day.

The difference between being aware of something and being in a state of hyperawareness is that when you have hyperawareness it is **directly linked to a goal** you have set. It keeps you present in every moment and creates constant urgency behind whatever goal you seek.

This elevated state of awareness in any given moment keeps you "in the now" and constantly excited about the goals you want to achieve. It is as if we have bottled up the initial excitement of hitting a goal, and keeping it for future times when we might be faltering on our commitments. This state will put you back on track in no time. There are a few simple ways to achieve this state of mind easily and regularly.

Once you have decided in your life what you want out of any particular area of your life you must constantly remind yourself of what you truly want and thus keep yourself on track. To do so is ridiculously simple.

You must constantly ground yourself with this simple question; **"Is what I am doing right now moving me closer to or further away from my goal?"** This is one of the most powerful questions you can learn to ask yourself on a regular basis. Constantly ask yourself if this is what you truly WANT, or is it just what you want right in the moment. Take a moment now to step out of the situation and check yourself.

Take into account the example used earlier about having a weight-loss goal and ending up going to a BBQ with friends to pig out. While you might be aware this is not a good decision, you may still go and pig out anyways. However, if you exercise hyperawareness and step back for a moment to ask yourself, is this moving me closer to or further away from my goal or in other words: *is what I am doing right this moment going to help or hurt me in pursuit of what I **TRULY** want? Is what I am doing right now helping me achieve a greater goal, or just giving me temporary pleasure?* Is eating this massive meal of meat and fat going to make me feel good about my goal, or simply feel good for the moments I am enjoying it?

Weigh what you know about the difference between pleasure and happiness. Another way of thinking of this question is to ask yourself: "Is what I am doing right now going to provide me with lasting happiness, or is it just something that will give me temporary pleasure?"

Hyperawareness is a simple tool we can all use on a daily basis that reels us back in to our goals when we are lead astray by distractions. It's a tool that is easily activated by one simple question: **Is what I am doing right now moving me closer to or further away from my goal?** My challenge to you is to ask yourself this question 10 times a day for the next 10 days. You will instantly see how easy it can make your day-to-day decision-making.

**ACTION STEP:** Ask yourself 10 times a day "Is what I am doing right now moving me closer to, or further away from my goals?"

# 4. THE SUCCESS CYCLE

**"Only those who will risk going too far can possibly find out how far they can go."**

**– T.S. Elliot, Best-selling author**

**"Energy & persistence conquer all things."**

> **– Benjamin Franklin, founding father of the United States**

**"One way to keep momentum going is to have constantly greater goals."**

> **– Michael Kodra, NY times best selling author**

The success cycle is one of the most important tools that you can identify and plug yourself into that will put you on the road to hitting your goals. It relies on three simple steps that can move equally in a positive or negative direction. It is up to you to identify your success cycle and use it to your advantage to breed bigger success in your life.

The three simple steps of the success cycle are as follows: Awareness, massive action, and results. This process is ongoing in many different aspects of your life and once you identify and value its power it will unlock anything you want to achieve. Also, you must be mindful that the success cycle can move in both a positive and negative direction.

Let's look at a few examples: First we will walk through the positive, and then I will show you how easy it can be to fall into a negative success cycle if you are not hyperaware of yourself and your surroundings. Say you have the desire to lose weight, or just generally improve your health—this will show you how understanding the success cycle along the way will aid your results.

The first key element of it is awareness, the identification of the issue. Becoming aware of an issue or situation is the first vital element to changing it. How many people do you know have goals, but do not achieve them simply because they do not know the major factors holding them back, or even the major factors that will allow them to overcome challenges?

In this example of weight loss, say you have a goal to lose 20 pounds by a certain date, or just to get in better shape (the more specific goal the better). You first use the success cycle to make you aware, or "hyperaware" of what you want. You become aware of the WHY behind what you want to achieve. In this first stage of awareness you must identify the major factors that might hold you back from hitting this goal. What are the key elements of what will get you to this goal faster and what will hold you back? Are you eating unhealthy food? Are you not exercising nearly as much as you know you should be? Are you associating in groups of people who are making unhealthy decisions? The first step in the success cycle is to become aware of all of these factors and use them to make a plan for success.

Awareness may come in stages, gradually or suddenly. Regardless of when you become aware of an issue, that is the first step in the success cycle. Awareness is a state that many people live in, but do not possess the desire to change. What I mean is that most people who are unhealthy are aware that this is an issue; however, they are not willing or able to change it at the moment.

In order to move forward in the success cycle the next step is crucial. MASSIVE ACTION. We must attack this new goal with all the force possible. This action can come in many different forms. Part of this massive action could include breaking down a plan that will help achieve the goal. It could also be immediate action towards the goal. The most important thing is that action is massive and immediate. It is important that the first move toward your goal be big and exciting. Use your "Why" to fuel your mission towards success. If it is something you truly want, then do not wait for it to come to you—go attack it with massive action.

To plug yourself into the success cycle means you need to live a life of integrity and not be making excuses. If you truly want success, you will be willing to take the massive action required to obtain it.

**"When you want to succeed as bad as you want to breathe, then you'll be successful."**

**– Eric Thomas, International keynote speaker and author**

## TAKE ACTION NOW!

Do not be afraid of "what if" situations. Take the jump towards success and learn to fly on your way down. Having a plan is great, but you must take immediate action. Don't wait to be great. Stop thinking about the thing you know should be doing and just do the positive thing you're thinking about. It is important for the action to be *massive,* because without massive action the success cycle cannot be fueled into the next step.

Get up right now and go to the gym. Turn off the TV and start working on your writing. Pick up the phone and make the call you know you should. Grab a pen and pad and start working on that project. Do whatever it is you need to do right NOW to move you closer to your goal.

When you decide to take massive action towards your goal you create the first spark in the success cycle.

The third step of this process is *results.* Results can be both positive and negative, but by taking MASSIVE ACTION you increase the chances that the results will breed a more positive result. Your big jump towards your goal is more likely to yield more positive results.

These positive results are the building blocks to the next success cycle. Take these positive results and use them to feel good about the work you have put in. Say your goal was to lose 20 pounds. You may have wanted to lose 4 the first week, but only lost 2.5. That is still very positive, because you are moving in a direction closer to your goal, not further away. Also, this is great because you can use these results to feed back into another success cycle.

After you get a result from the success cycle it's time to feed that result back into another state of awareness and start the cycle over again. Each success cycle builds off of the previous one and that creates a wave of momentum that cannot be stopped.

Two important factors to realize about this cycle. The first is that it is constant. One cycle feeds into the next, and there is no stopping in between. One of the single biggest killers of goals is loss of momentum. The key to using and thriving in the success cycle is to keep it going constantly. Always be hyperaware of the goals you want to achieve and the date you want to do them by. Do not allow pauses between getting results and using those results to obtain even better results. The success cycle is a feedback loop that can be your best friend or worst enemy.

The other major element of the success cycle that you must learn is that the speed and magnitude of the cycle will be a direct reflection of the massive action you take towards it. "Massive Action" can be interpreted all types of ways for all different types of people. The speed at which the cycle grows or slows is completely up to the operator. To yield the best result the best cycles are done faster. The swifter you can go through it the larger the momentum.

## SUCCESS IS A NEVER-ENDING TWO-WAY STREET

Another key component is that the cycle can be both positive and negative. A negative cycle can yield as much damage as positive results. For example, someone is aware of a weight problem they have, but they take no action towards it. This lack of action creates a negative result. This negative result has the ability to cut off any future growth of positive goals. If not corrected, a negative success cycle can be catastrophic to you and your health. So many people today are caught in negative success cycles, and seldom have a way out.

The good news is that no matter how negative the cycle feels it can be switched by taking one positive success cycle. Even if the results are not that large, the direction of momentum has been changed. A simple state of awareness and massive action are all you need to break free of a long-standing negative success cycle.

Take a different example of getting good grades in school, or in most cases breaking the negative success cycle of getting bad grades. In order to change these results, you must first identify the things that are holding you back from hitting them, and also what simple changes you could be making in order to achieve these goals. Many of the questions you ask yourself could be similar: What are my daily school work habits? Am I associating with people who do not value the same things that I do? Am I making progress every day towards this goal, or am I gradually letting it slip away like I have with many goals in the past?

## 5. Live life with "NO EXCUSES"

Don't make excuses for the person you know you want to be. I would like to share a story with you of a profound life event I experienced. I was going to the gym one night in 2012. It was a Saturday night around 10PM in late January. A time of the year where all the "new year's resolutioners" had siphoned off, so the gym was no longer very busy.

At this point in my life I was living what most people would consider a relatively healthy lifestyle. I had lost 60 pounds, learned a lot about health and fitness, got a good job and was about to graduate from college. To the outside world, life was good for Eric.

Have you ever felt like you can be doing much more, but you get so caught up in life that you make excuses for why you cannot take your life to the next level? Although I was healthy, I still strived to take my fitness to a higher level. They say to lose "the last 10 pounds" is the hardest, and this was true for me. Ever since high school I was on a path of growth in my fitness level, but I had never taken it to the extreme. I was doing just enough to get back and maintain, but not push myself further; that all changed that night in January when I walked into the gym.

I was in the gym, which was pretty quiet, doing my normal workout, when I saw a man walk in who looked a bit odd. I say this because of what he was wearing. It wasn't the normal gym clothes that most people wear. He was wearing full medical scrubs, like from a hospital.

Intrigued by his outfit, I casually walked over and introduced myself. He was about 6'1" and appeared to be in pretty good shape. He had a shaved head and an inviting smile. He seemed nice enough to ask a question. I told him that I just had to ask, "What's up with the scrubs? Are you like in between shifts or something right now, or going to work soon?"

He chuckled a bit and said, "I figured someone might ask about it. You know, I actually just got off a 16-hour shift at the hospital. I have been up since 5AM (It was around 10:30PM). But, you know what Eric, this year, 2012, I told myself "No Excuses." Every day I go to the gym, no matter what. I knew that if I went home to change I would make up some excuse for why I can't make it here, and that's not happening."

I told him that I was very impressed and I would let him get back to his workout. We parted ways, never to meet again, but the imprint he left on my life will last forever.

It was a few minutes later when I was on another machine, in between sets, looking across the gym at my new inspirational friend, that it all hit me like a slap in the face. "NO EXCUSES!" The only reason we are not where we want to be in our lives is because of the excuses we throw in front of ourselves. Excuses distract us from the person we want to be and know we are capable of being.

We are all guilty of making excuses at some point in our lives, and I would bet that if you look back upon your own experiences that excuses have held you back in some way, shape or form. You must *not* let excuses deter you from the person you want to become.

There is also a difference between an excuse and a reason. Simply put, reasons are external and excuses are internal. Reasons are somewhat legitimate, but they come from circumstances out of your control. Far more commonly, the "reason" we don't do something is because of an excuse we make up, fabricated out of our own mind.

Here is a quick example. You have a goal to get to work on time and 10 minutes before you get into your car someone comes and steals it. This would be a reason you could no longer get to work on time, because something external out of your control deterred you.

More commonly, people would be late for work, blame it on their bad alarm clock, the traffic, the long line at Starbucks and the fact that they overslept. These are all ways to manufacture your own excuses for not doing something you said you would.

**Key point: Integrity means keeping your word. Doing everything you said you were going to do, when you say you will do it, without exceptions or excuses.**

Most of the time we don't achieve something we want is because of the B.S. excuses we put in front of ourselves. Now is the time to stop making excuses, accept responsibility for your own results and create the life of your dreams through making healthy choices.

It was later in that week, after meeting my new friend in the gym that I got a bracelet made. It was a small metal coin on a string with the words "NO EXCUSES" hammered into it. I wore it every single day as a constant reminder to not make excuses for the person I want to become.

I have since updated it to a rubber bracelet that is much more durable. I never take it off. In fact, I wear two of them: one facing inwards so I can read it and one facing outwards, so others can read it. When people ask me about it I share the story with them and if they want I will give them the 2$^{nd}$ bracelet. I would like to share that opportunity with you as well. I want to share this incredibly simple and powerful message with as many people as possible. It has served me and so many others to be a constant reminder to not make excuses. If you would like a bracelet simply find my "Eric Gillman" Facebook page, like the page and send me a message with your mailing address and email. I will send you two "NO EXCUSES" bracelets absolutely free! This is a simple message that we can use to change the world and I want to share it with as many people as possible.

Whenever the voice in the back of your head creeps in and tries to distract you from your true goal, just look down at that bracelet and tell yourself, "NO EXCUSES." You are no longer the person who is going to make excuses for the life you know you are capable and deserving of living.

# CHAPTER 9
# KAIZEN: Constant and Never Ending Improvement

"Every day a little bit stronger, a little bit smarter, a little bit better. Make every day the best day of my life."

– Eric Gillman

"For changes to be of any true value, they've got to be lasting and consistent."

– Tony Robbins, International Keynote speaker

"What lies behind us and what lies before us are tiny compared to what lies within us"

– Ralph Waldo Emerson, Lecturer, author and speaker

It is exciting to have big goals and big things to go for. To find a why and pursue it with passion is one of the greatest journeys you can have. It's important to have big goals and go for them, but we must learn to make *every* day the best day of our lives, and enjoy the process of pursuing the goal. The journey on the way to your goal is the real satisfaction of the goal.

As we discussed before, the true purpose of a goal is not

necessarily to hit the goal, but to become the person you will become by pursuing that goal with everything that you have. The goal itself is merely the finish line; it is the icing on the cake.

**"Success is not a destination, but the journey you take to get there."**
**– Eric Gillman**

At some point during my life I learned a very valuable lesson that I want to share with you today. It is that in our minds we paint an image of what success will feel like. What you will achieve out of hitting a certain goal or a mark that you desire. While these moments of achievement can be some of the best of your life, the true success you will experience is the journey that you take to get there. As mentioned before—and it must be repeated because its impact is real—the most important part of a goal is not the goal itself, but the journey you take to get you there. The thousands of healthy choices you make in an effort achieve this goal.

As we discussed previously, goals are never static. We are always moving closer to or further away from a goal. The more we can be aware, or hyperaware of this circumstance, the more in control of the goal's direction we become. The key factor in the pursuit of a goal or dream is that you never stop moving towards it. It is always something in your mind that you are working towards.

The Japanese have a word for this: Kaizen. (The Japanese character is 改善) Kaizen translates to *constant improvement*. It is the concept that you are always working on improving something, someone, or yourself. The key word here is *constant*. A constant is defined in science as "something that is always there." It never goes away, and is always the same.

Your goal must be a constant in your mind. It must be something you are always working towards improving. Sometimes it might not be the most important thing you have to do in the moment, but it is always something that is on your mind—it is a constant in your consciousness.

The great thing about making your goal and desires a constant in your mind is that you will have no choice but to work on improving them. If there is something you truly want out of life, and you constantly and consciously remind yourself of it, then you will inevitably start aligning your actions with what you want. However, you MUST first constantly remind yourself of what you want, and the rest will follow.

So there I was, just signed up to do my first half marathon, 13.1 miles! Why did I do it? I don't really know. My friend challenged me, and I am never one to back down from a challenge, even if I don't know how I will overcome it. I knew that doing something like this would help me grow into the person I wanted to become.

Have you ever committed to something without having the slightest clue of how you were going to accomplish the task? Jumped into a situation without any idea what you're doing, like jumping into the deep end of a pool, and then trying to learn how to swim?

It was time for me to step up and get cracking on this goal, so I did the only thing I knew I could do: I started running. I started doing what I could do. I put one foot in front of the other, again and again until I couldn't continue.

In life, when you commit to something you don't really know how to do, there is only one thing to do: focus on what you do know how to do. I didn't know how to train properly. I knew little about the finesse of running, or the complexities of stretching. I just started to run. No one is great at anything the first time they ever try it, so you have to start somewhere and just put one foot in front of the other, no matter what the task ahead is.

Bit by bit, every day I felt myself getting a little bit faster, and a little bit stronger. I wasn't even sure what the expected outcome should or would be, I just knew to put one foot in front of the other and keep going until I couldn't go anymore.

As the preparation continued I felt myself getting more and more confident in my skills. I stopped making excuses why I couldn't do things, and started giving myself reasons why I should.

It is imperative that you constantly improve yourself in all areas of your life. Your path to greatness doesn't have to be drastic and quick, although it could be, but if you focused on constant and never ending improvement you will always be moving closer to the person you want to become.

If your goal is to run more, start with what you can do now and add on just a bit every day. If your goal is to read more, but you can't read more than 5 pages without getting distracted, start with that and add a page every day. If your goal is to be a more outgoing person, start by pushing yourself outside your comfort zone at least once at a day. Practicing the concept of Kaizen, constant and never ending improvement will always leave you closer to your goals than when you started.

I sought the help of others who had walked my path before and were willing and able to offer some advice. I learned from my mistakes and allowed them to make me a better person along the way. I was able to embrace the journey and allow it to open my life to something that I never knew before: that I actually enjoy running for long distances. How can you ever know if you truly like or dislike something if you have never tried it before?

Kaizen is the constant and never-ending improvement that we should all strive towards. Sometimes that means taking two steps forward and one back, but the point is that you will find yourself further along your path to success if you always focus on constant and never-ending improvement, no matter how big or small.

You must have the bad days in your life in order to appreciate the good ones.

## RACE DAY: Failure to Launch

So I continued to train. Days turned into weeks, weeks turned into months, and before I knew it, the race was right around the corner. I felt as ready as I could be, and knew I was prepared to give it my all. I had done everything in my power to make sure I was ready, and now it was the night before the race.

I knew I had to be up at 5:45AM to get to the race in time and start at 7:30AM. So I got everything prepared for the race. I had my big dinner of carbs and veggies to fuel me up for the race and I laid my head on my pillow at about 11PM. I tossed and turned for a while in excited anticipation of the morning to come.

I awoke to the sound of an alarm going off, and I rolled over in my bed. I knew immediately something was off because it was far too light in my room. I turned over to look at the clock on my phone—it was 7:30AM!

I felt like I had been punched in the heart and gut at the same time. I sprang out of bed like a frog in a panic. I didn't know what to do. For a few brief moments I scrambled around my apartment hoping this was some type of bad dream.

It was not.

After all the preparation, overcoming my own attitude and getting ready physically and mentally, I'd slept through my alarm and missed the start of the race.

I gathered myself and called one of my life's best mentors, my dad. I called him up and he answered by saying, "So you must be right about to run the race?"

I told him that I overslept and I didn't know what to do. All this time getting ready, all this training and preparation, seemingly down the drain. All this work seemed washed away by the sound of my tardy alarm clock.

My dad, always one to embrace the process and look on the bright side of things, gave me the encouraging push I needed in that moment. He said, "Well, you spent all this time preparing, just go! Go now!" Without even giving myself any time to think I grabbed my bag, got dressed and was out the door in less than two minutes.

The starting point of the race was about a 15–20 minute drive. I made it there in 10 minutes. I arrived at the local fairgrounds, the starting point, at about 8:15. I showed up to find an abandoned parking lot, occupied solely by a maintenance crew that was taking down the speakers to announce the start of the race.

In a revisiting of my panic I asked the crew guys, "Where is everybody?" to which they told me, they all have left. I felt a deep sense of disappointment sink over me, like I had missed my ship to freedom. So much time put into preparing for this race, but I wasn't willing to let it all die there, in the parking lot of the Del Mar Fairgrounds.

Another great mentor of mine once told me to be successful you must learn to respond to situations, not react to them. This was a situation in which I could have reacted: given up right there, thrown in the towel and went home in disappointment.

In the process of achieving goals you must sometimes take a step backwards between every step or two forwards. Kaizen means to be constantly moving towards one's goal, and embracing the process along the way. In that moment, standing in the fairgrounds parking lot I had to make a choice. I could give up on everything I had worked towards, or, at the very least, run the race I had been looking forward to so much. I chose to respond and not react to my mistake.

I looked at the crewman and I said, "Which way did they go!"

He pointed and I took off running. I knew I wasn't going to finish in the exact time I wanted to, but damn it, I was going to finish this race. Success isn't always about the destination and the goal itself, but the person you become in the process of pursuing such a goal.

As I took off running I was alone for the first 4 or 5 miles. I came down a small hill and then I saw her. I was so excited to see her. Who was she? She was the lady who was in the very last place in the race. A seventy-something-year-old woman, power-walking by herself, followed right behind by the end of the race crew, picking up the cones and markers behind her as she finished the race.

I remember thinking, at least I won't be the very last person to finish. After her I started to see more and more people as I breezed through the back of the pack. First it was the elderly groups of walkers, then the power walkers, then the groups of not very well-trained joggers, then the runners. One by one I passed my way up to people who were actually running. I remember thinking how exciting it was that I was actually going to finish this race. I knew it wasn't going to be in my goal of under two hours, but at least I was going to finish.

According to the official race time I finished in 3 hours, but nothing was clocked officially. I got my medal at the end, and took my long trip home. I felt good that I at least completed the race, but not at all in the fashion I had hoped for.

I went home that night, did a little research and found out that there was another half-marathon in my town the very next weekend. Feeling obligated to embrace the process, I signed up for the race.

The night before I got everything ready, set 5 alarms and made sure to do everything to make sure I was up on time. I woke up five minutes before the clock went off, got ready and ran my race. I finished with a time of 1:59:03, less than a minute under my goal.

At first I might have not seen the big picture of it all, but missing my first marathon was all part of the process. It's important to embrace all the days, both good and bad. You can't appreciate the good days without the bad—as we now know, kaizen means embracing the process of constant and never-ending improvement.

Success is a constant and never-ending process, for which you must be willing and able to embrace every step along the way.

Visualize the person you want to be in the future. Ask yourself constantly, what would that person do in this situation? When you have a clear image of the person you want to become then you can use that to guide you through your daily actions, in an effort to eventually become that person.

The goal for some people might seem like the entire prize, or the final destination, but this is not true. The goal is to show you, and the rest of the world, that you can endure and outlast the process, whatever process that may be. Hitting a goal is simply the culmination of the process, so it is best to enjoy the process.

**People are rewarded in public for the work they do in private.**

When a student graduates from high school or college they are given a graduation ceremony in front of everyone. They are rewarded with a diploma, but the diploma is merely the symbol. The symbol of the countless hours of reading, studying, researching and testing that the student did by themselves.

Hitting big goals is not easy, and no one ever said it is. There is no choice of easy or hard way to do legendary things; there is only the hard way. The only choice you have is how you choose to deal with it. Will you choose to gripe and groan until you can't go on anymore, like so many who try to achieve great things? Or will you choose to embrace the process of growth? Choose to take the hard road over the easy road, because you know you will grow more.

You only get one chance to live your life, so embrace each day as if it could be your last. What if today was your last day on earth? How would you act? What would you do?

Your time on this earth is limited, but we are all put here with unlimited potential. You are just as worthy, capable and deserving of achieving your goals as any other person on this planet. The only thing that separates successful people from unsuccessful people is their willingness to put in the conscious and intentional effort to pursue their goals.

After doing the exercises earlier in this book you should have a pretty good idea of something you want to achieve in your life. If it is still unclear, I encourage you to flip back through to chapter 7 and complete the exercises again. Don't be afraid to think big and go for big things. Nothing big in this world ever came from people thinking small. It comes from people thinking big and failing forward towards their goals.

Don't be afraid to shoot for big goals and fail. No matter how bad you fail, you will still be further ahead of where you were before you started. Constant and never-ending improvement will force you to become the person you desire to be.

Who is that person, and what can you do to become that person?

# CHAPTER 10
# Do It Now!

**"There is no better time in your life to take action than right now."**

**– Tony Robbins, International Keynote speaker**

**"We are who we are because of the choices we have made in the past, but where we are going depends completely upon the choices you make today."**

**– Hal Elrod, International Keynote speaker and NY Times best-selling author**

So, now that you have the tools and you have the vision, what are you waiting for? There is no better time in your life to take action than right now. Don't make excuses for the person that you know you want to be.

Far too often we get caught up in our day-to-day lives and we allow excuses to overwhelm us and distract us from what we truly want out of life. What every person wants out of life is different, but we all desire something. We are born with it. It is the desire in your heart and the voice in the back of your head that drives you to become a better version of yourself. It was that same voice within you that drove you to pick up this book and start reading.

Now that you have completed this book (way to go!), it is time to put it to work. Don't wait to be great. Right now, as soon as you finish the book, *take action.* Strike while the iron is hot. Do something that is going to move you closer to the person you want to become, in any area of your life. You know what you want, so what are you waiting for? Take the first step right now. Ask yourself, "Is what I am doing right now moving me closer to, or further away from my goal?"

You know your mountaintop: right now is the best time to take a powerful step in the direction of the peak. You have everything you need within you—USE IT!

Human beings are capable of achieving incredible things. The history books are filled with exceptional people who rose up to create something more with their lives. The secret is that they are no better than you, or me, or for that matter, any other person. They simply embraced chances to grow into greater people and seized opportunities that they had.

You are just as worthy, capable and deserving to live the life of your dreams as any other person. In order to be ready to do so you must prepare by making healthy choices every day that are going to lead you to be the person who can achieve your goals.

When preparation meets opportunity, then amazing things happen.

# Notable Quotes Section

If you are like me and love to hear and see inspiring things on a regular basis, then here is a section of the book which you can use regularly. This is a compilation of the inspiring quotes used throughout the entire book. Please feel free to remove these pages, copy them and post them up everywhere in your house, car, office, or wherever you feel they can benefit you. Use them to stay dedicated to the goals you have set for yourself.

Thank you so much for investing the time to read my book. I am truly grateful for it and I hope I can continue to add value to your life in any way possible. You are an extraordinary person who is a capable of changing the world through your actions!

"There's no reason to have a plan B because it distracts from plan A."

— Will Smith, two-time Academy Award winning actor

"To make a decision means to cut off the other option. Once you have truly harnessed the power of a decision, the other option no longer exists."

— Eric Gillman

"You miss 100% of the shots you don't take."
                    – Wayne Gretzky, Ice Hockey legend and MVP


"You must do the thing you think you cannot do"
                    – Eleanor Roosevelt, Former first lady of the United States


"Success is not final, failure is not fatal: it is the courage to continue that counts."
– Winston Churchill, Former Prime Minister of the United Kingdom


"There is no such thing as failure. There are only results."
                    – Tony Robbins, International motivational speaker


"You are just as worthy, deserving, and capable of achieving everything you want as any other person on earth."
                    – Hal Elrod, International Keynote speaker
                    and NY Times best-selling author


"I've missed more than 9,000 shots in my career. I've lost almost 300 games. Twenty-six times, I've been trusted to take the game winning shot and missed. I've failed over and over and over again in my life. And that is why I succeed."
                    – Michael Jordan, six-time NBA champion
                    and five-time NBA MVP


"There are no secrets to success. It is the result of preparation, hard work and learning from failure"
                    – Colin Powell, Former Secretary General of the United States


"The difference between a successful person and others is not a lack of strength, not a lack of knowledge, but rather in a lack of will."
                    – Vince Lombardi, Hall of Fame NFL coaching legend

"You can achieve everything you want out of life, once you help enough people achieve what they want out of life."

– Eric Gillman

"Where you are is a result of who you were, but where you go depends entirely on who you choose to be."

– Hal Elrod, International Keynote speaker and NY Times best-selling author

"The moment you accept responsibility for everything in your life is the moment you gain the power to change anything in your life."

– Hal Elrod, International Keynote speaker and NY Times best-selling author

"Don't let the things that you can't do affect the things that you can do."

– Matthew Kelly, International Keynote speaker and NY Times best-selling author

"Success consists of going from failure to failure without a loss of enthusiasm."

- Winston Churchill, Former Prime Minister of the UK

"Never be afraid to fail, be afraid of not learning from your mistakes."

- Unknown

"Let food be thy medicine."

– Hippocrates, ancient philosopher

"Every moment of success is built upon a mountainous foundation of failure before it."

– Eric Gillman

"Take care of your body. It's the only place you have to live."

– Jim Rohn, International keynote speaker, author and coach

–

"To make a decision means to cut off the other option. Once you have truly harnessed the power of a decision, the other option no longer exists."

– Eric Gillman

"What some folks call impossible, is just stuff they haven't seen before."

– *What Dreams May Come*

"The moment you tell yourself you "Can't" do something, is the moment you rob yourself of the divine feeling it is to achieve something."

– Eric Gillman

"If you always put limits on everything you do, physical or anything else, it will spread into your work and into your life. There are no limits. There are only plateaus; and you must not stay there, you must go beyond them."

–Bruce Lee, Martial arts legend

"What is the best way to eat an elephant? One bite at a time"

– Unknown

DO WHAT"S RIGHT, NOT WHAT'S EASY"

-Eric Gillman

"There's no traffic on the extra mile"
> – Rickey Minor, International music director

"Is what I am doing right now moving me closer to or further away from my goal?"
> – Eric Gillman

"Only those who will risk going to far can possibly find out how far they can go"
> – T.S. Elliot, Best-selling author

"Energy & persistence conquer all things."
> – Benjamin Franklin, founding father of the United States

"When you want to succeed as bad as you want to breathe, then you'll be successful."
> – Eric Thomas, International keynote speaker and author

"Every day a little bit stronger, a little bit smarter, a little bit better. Make every day the best day of my life."
> – Eric Gillman

"For changes to be of any true value, they've got to be lasting and consistent."
> – Tony Robbins, International motivational speaker

"One way to keep momentum going is to have constantly greater goals."
> – Michael Kodra, NY times best selling author

"What lies behind us and what lies before us are tiny compared to what lies within us"
— Ralph Waldo Emerson, Lecturer, author and speaker

"Success is not a destination, but the journey you take to get there."
— Eric Gillman

"There is no better time in your life to take action than right now."
— Tony Robbins, International motivational speaker

"We are who we are because of the choices we have made in the past, but where we are going depends completely upon the choices you make today."
— Hal Elrod, International Keynote speaker and NY Times best-selling author

# Notes

# Notes

# Notes

# Notes

# Notes

# Notes

# <u>SET YOUR GOALS TODAY!</u>

MY BIGGEST GOAL IS

_____

MY NEXT STEP TOWARDS MY GOAL **TODAY** IS

_____

## SUMMARY AND WORK PAGE:

- I WANT TO ACCOMPLISH _____ IN MY LIFE!

- TO ACCOMPLISH _____WOULD MEAN

  _____

- MY BIGGEST GOAL IS

  _____

- MY NEXT STEP TOWARDS MY GOAL **TODAY** IS_____

- I WILL ACCOMPLISH _____ BY _____!

# About the Author

Eric Gillman is a Hall of Fame sales professional in a quarter billion-dollar marketing company, an accomplished marathon runner, and motivational speaker, but it wasn't always that way. A troubled and unhealthy teenager, Eric was able to turn his life around using some simple techniques which he now wants to share with everyone. It is his mission in life to inspire people of the world to become the best version of themselves by helping them make the healthy choices that will allow them to achieve what they want in life. Eric teaches simple strategies that lead to a happy and healthy experience in any area of your life. If you would like more information about the author, or to inquire about having Eric speak to your audience, please visit his website at EricGillman.com.

Made in the USA
Monee, IL
15 May 2021